Conquer
Change and Win

Conquer
Change and Win

**AN EASY-TO-READ, FUN BOOK ABOUT THE
SERIOUS SUBJECT OF CHANGE**

Ralph Masengill, Jr.

Contents

Introduction · vii

Chapter 1   What Is Change? · 1

Chapter 2   The 20-50-30 Rule · 9

Chapter 3   Resistance to Change · · · · · · · · · · · · · · · · · · · 12

Chapter 4   How to Deal with Difficult People · · · · · · · · · · · · 16

Chapter 5   Attitude and Change · 21

Chapter 6   Positive and Negative Change · · · · · · · · · · · · · · 31

Chapter 7   Fear and Anxiety Caused by Change · · · · · · · · · · · · 37

Chapter 8   Risk of Change or Supposed Security · · · · · · · · · · · 51

Chapter 9   Managing the Stress Caused by Change · · · · · · · · · · 58

Chapter 10 Decision-Making During Change · · · · · · · · · · · · · · 65

Chapter 11 Problem-Solving During Change: Understanding
            Leads to Solving the Problem · · · · · · · · · · · · · · · · 77

Chapter 12   Communication and Change-Management · · · · · · · · ·80

Chapter 13   How to Motivate and Sell People on Change · · · · · · · ·89

Chapter 14   The Art of Negotiation ·97

Chapter 15   The Anatomy of a Great Change Agent · · · · · · · · · · ·108

Chapter 16   How to Build a Winning Change Team· · · · · · · · · · · ·113

Chapter 17   Creating the Best Change-Management Plan Possible · ·119

Chapter 18   Vision, Mission, and Current-Reality Statements of
the Change-Management Plan · · · · · · · · · · · · · · · · ·130

Chapter 19   Changing the Original Change-Management Plan · · ·139

Chapter 20   Implementing the Change-Management Plan· · · · · · ·142

Chapter 21   Managing Change Management· · · · · · · · · · · · · · · ·152

Chapter 22   Conclusion ·156

Appendix ·159

About the Author ·165

Introduction

Change is inevitable—except from a vending machine.
—ROBERT C. GALLAGHER

This fun, educational book will show you how to win more consistently by understanding change. Understanding how change works will enhance your success. How change makes you and others feel is something few are aware of in the twenty-first century. You will learn how to react to and control the feelings that the emotions of change always cause. The information in this book will make positive change work for you and put you ahead of the curve.

Change management is a frequent target of academic study today. Some thinkers in the academic arena and others try to reinvent change management every three to five years. Mostly, they simply change the names of principles or points and maybe add a twist or two. This is one reason why the how-to of change management is often garbled and confusing. I'll cut through the haze and show you the best ways to manage both positive and negative change.

Change is a mystery to most people—one that can and does defeat many. This book will show you how to be an exception to the rule. You will have a leg up on more than 90 percent of the people in the United States. The information in this book has been a major key to my success and enhanced happiness, both in my personal life and in running my businesses. Understanding change is a keystone to that arch called success. You will learn to make positive change.

There are so many misconceptions about the way change works. This book reveals the truth. It teaches in commonsense English the fastest and best ways to approach change in your personal life and in your business.

You will be in a better position to make large and small decisions. You will become more confident in your decision-making ability. You will learn how change affects your emotions, regardless of whether the change is positive or negative. The key to getting the most out of this book is to sit back and have fun as you learn more about a complicated and important subject.

Understanding change is not difficult, but it does take effort and time to understand the various kinds of change and the effects that change can have on emotions. Sometimes the hardest thing in learning about change is believing that the facts are true. When you believe that the facts about change are indeed valid and do affect you in predictable ways, then you will come away with a solid understanding of change and how to make it work for you every day.

Understanding change can help you become more likeable. It does; it really does. My wife tells me that this is her favorite consequence of me studying change all these years. I think what she said was a compliment—or does it mean that when we first met, I was unlikeable?

This book is about making you a true winner, a better leader, and a consistently happier person. Let's take an interesting and fun journey into the serious world of change.

CHAPTER 1

What Is Change?

Most of us will not change until the pain of not changing
is greater than the pain of changing.
— ANONYMOUS

Change became a passion of mine in the late sixties and early seventies. Understanding change has made a difference in my life and my businesses. A lot of things must come together for true success to occur, and one of them in today's world is understanding change.

The old saying goes that two things are certain in life: death and taxes. But that old saying leaves out one more certainty: change. No matter how hard we try, we cannot avoid change. If we cannot escape going through change, then we must learn all we can about this certainty of life. Few people on earth have a good working knowledge of change and how it affects them. Understanding both positive and negative change is one of the secrets of being happy and wealthy.

Do you want to be successful? Here is the simple secret. You will be a true winner only if you do these three things:

1. Take a calculated risk and endorse change on a regular basis.
2. Learn how change affects your emotions, along with those of the people around you.

3. Know how to react to the feelings that the emotions of change always bring with them.

We humans—and there are no exceptions—are constantly involved in change. It never stops; it continues constantly in and around us. Change cannot be stopped, but it can be controlled. Our job is to control the feelings that the emotions of change bring.

Are you in a personal or business rut? If you are, you have no control over where that rut will take you. You have lost your freedom to act. Staying in a rut will cost you the freedom to control your life, your business, or both. Laurence J. Peter states, "A rut is a grave with the ends knocked out." He's talking about living life without understanding the importance of the effects that change has on all of us on a daily basis.

Mark Twain put it this way: "Twenty years from now, you will be more disappointed by the things you didn't do than by the ones you did do. So throw off the bowlines. Sail away from the safe harbor." Many good people refuse to accept the risk and uncertainty that change brings. They stay in self-imposed ruts. They force themselves to live in stagnant prisons of their own making. They do have part of it right, though. There can be some security in a prison. With change you have two choices: one is to embrace change with gusto, and the other is to stay in a rut by refusing to admit that change is constant. Those who choose ruts live in denial. Because of their bad choices, they end up losing the freedom to act. The solution is to simply agree to devote time and effort to understanding change and how it makes you feel. You have done that. So, congratulations.

One old saying goes, "Life isn't about how to survive the storm but how to dance in the rain." I believe the happiest and most successful people do not necessarily have the best of everything; they just make the best of everything they have. Choose to understand change. It is a path to more personal happiness and business success.

If that is true, what is change? How does change affect all of us on a continuous basis? After forty years of study and research, here is my definition of change:

CHANGE

Doing something different. All men and women regard all change —both good and bad—with a feeling of loss (examples would be remorse or that pit-of-the-stomach feeling), and that feeling of loss always creates some form of anxiety, anger, or fear.

Understanding how change works can change your life for the better and give you a solid advantage. That's a guarantee. Here are some interesting facts about continuous change to get us on our way:

1. Most of us will not change until the pain of not changing is greater than the pain of changing.
2. Most people often prefer the security of known misery to the supposed misery of unfamiliar insecurity.
3. Change is continual—intended or not.

Number one on the list above was once true for me in a big way. Before I learned how to handle continuous change and understand the effect change had on my personality, nothing seemed to get better. I seemed stuck in a continuous rut. Understanding continuous change turned my humdrum life around. To understand change, you must work at it continuously.

What do others say about change?

They always say time changes things, but you actually have to change them yourself.
—ANDY WARHOL

Only I can change my life. No one can do it for me.
—CAROL BURNETT

Change your thoughts, and you change your world.
—NORMAN VINCENT PEALE

Nothing endures but change.
—HERACLITUS

Nobody can go back and start a new beginning, but anyone can start today and make a new ending, if you are willing to change.
—MARIA ROBINSON

I have accepted fear as part of life, specifically the fear of change…I have gone ahead despite the pounding in the heart that says: turn back.
—ERICA JONG

Nothing is as painful to the human mind as a great and sudden change.
—MARY SHELLEY

A corporation is a living organism; it has to continue to shed its skin. Methods have to change. Focus has to change. Values have to change. The sum total of those changes is transformation.
—ANDREW GROVE

He who rejects change is the architect of decay.
—HAROLD WILSON

Deep down, no one likes dealing with change. However, we all like the results of what we see as positive change. We often are in pain because of continuous change; our resistance to change will also cause us pain. The sooner we stop resisting the positive changes that happen in our lives and accept those changes, the sooner we have the opportunity to feel less stress and set our business and personal lives up for even more success. To be truly successful in any undertaking, you must embrace positive change and the pain resistance brings. You must do this willingly and often.

We accept risk every day when we embrace positive change. Do you take a calculated risk, or do you sometimes just roll the dice and hope for the best? I admit that in my younger days, I did more rolling of the dice than I want to talk about, and I had to pay the price. I paid the price by losing time, money, and happiness. Many times this was out of my own ignorance about change. One time, I almost lost my business. But we can learn from our mistakes. Mistakes can be good teachers. However, I have found that this is a very expensive and painful way to learn.

Charles Tremper puts it this way: "The first step in the calculated risk process is to acknowledge the reality of the risk. Denial is a common tactic that substitutes deliberate ignorance for thoughtful planning." I have a T-shirt that says, "Denial is not a river in Egypt." Denial is one way to delay. It is like the ostrich putting its head in the sand. Denial is one way to attempt to live in fantasy land.

Executing any plan involves change. Being willing to change is a calculated risk that should be encouraged. Most business and personal success in today's world comes when we accept this risk.

Let's talk about risk versus supposed security. Is security the opposite of risk? Some say it is, but I believe those people are in error. Here is what Helen Keller had to say about security: "Security is mostly a superstition. It does not exist in nature, nor do the children of men as a whole experience it. Avoiding danger is no safer in the long run than outright exposure. Life is either a daring adventure or nothing." Former President Eisenhower said, "One can find outright security only in a prison. In order to be absolutely secure, you must give up your in-dividual freedoms." In one of his lectures, Denis Waitley said, "Life is inherently risky. To become the success you want to be, there is only one big risk you should avoid at all cost. That is the risk of doing nothing." I believe total security is a myth.

Without calculated risk and the positive change it can bring, there would be no United States of America and no free-enterprise system. Our free-enterprise system is based on planned change that requires risk. This then creates an opportunity that can lead to a solid reward. Risk and change are things we should get up with gladly every morning. To succeed beyond even our most daring dreams, we must be willing to accept calculated risk and change as a way of life.

The following story delivers what I believe is an important change concept:

Imagine two ships sailing in opposite directions. One is going north, and the other is going south. However, the wind is blowing east. This can happen because of the way the captain sets the sails. The captain of each vessel has control of how the sails are set. It is always your choice which way you go. You have control of the set of the sails on your ship. It is never necessary to follow the wind, which you cannot control. By setting the sails correctly, you can choose your direction. You have control. You are the captain of your ship.

We have all seen or read about a business that does well in a cer-tain market while its competitor, offering the same product or service, flounders. Please take a moment right now and reread the above short story.

Now, make sure you know how the market winds are blowing. Then, and only then, set your business or personal sails accordingly. Use posi-tive change and take the calculated risk that is an integral part of the package. Do that correctly, and you can assuredly reach your destination of enhanced sales and profit, a better life, or both. You can then taste sweet success over and over.

Again, the first step is to know the direction of the market winds. Get this wrong, and all your other efforts do not matter. Over the years,

I have been amazed at how little time and money people spend on effective market research. Hunches have a place in the business sea, but it is not in this first step. Accurate market research is one of the first steps to enhancing your business profit or improving your personal or family life or both. You must react to the market. You must change to win. Judge the market winds right based on solid research; then begin to make the correct changes. Analytics (research) is an often misunderstood and misused tool.

You must work hard not to resist positive change. The solution is simple but not easy. Enhanced success is about learning all you can about change and how it makes you feel and being willing to take a calculated risk. Knowing what to expect when you need to change will help you be all that you want to be in this world. Work hard to see positive change as a friend, and do not resist this widely misunderstood process. Positive change is just that—positive. Embrace it, and you have a great opportunity to succeed, far above your present goals and dreams. Understanding change is well worth the effort and pain required.

Perhaps that sounds too simple. Well, it is no simple matter to judge the winds of the market correctly. This is where many well-capitalized companies lose the battle. If you do not know from which direction the market wind is blowing, then all your efforts to set your business sails correctly will fail—no matter how much time and money you invest. The same is true in your personal life.

In today's world, you must be able to separate the various myths about change from the facts you will find in this and other books. Misconceptions about change are rampant. Mark Twain said it this way: "It ain't what you don't know that gets you into trouble. It's what you know for sure that just is not so."

When you have a good understanding of change, both positive and negative, you will be in a solid position to win big in today's constantly changing world. You will simultaneously be in a super position to be happier as a person.

The list that follows in the box might be short, but this list is vital to business and personal success.

WAYS TO MORE HAPPINESS AND WEALTH

1. Take Calculated Risk.

2. Endorse Positive Change on a Regular Basis.

3. Know How Change Affects Your Emotions.

Understanding people's reaction to change can be explained by a very helpful and significant rule that will be discussed in the next chapter.

CHAPTER 2

The 20-50-30 Rule

It is not the strongest of the species that survives,
nor the most intelligent, but the one most responsive to change.
—CHARLES DARWIN

The rule states that 20 percent of your group or staff is going to be change friendly, 50 percent will be neutral (the wait-and-see folks), and 30 percent will be resisters. The 20-50-30 Rule has been around a long time. It is the truth very well told. Unfortunately, those who do not believe it are missing out on a lot of wisdom. I have found it to apply to every situation where accurate data has allowed me to measure such things. This rule has proven invaluable to me over the years. One reason some do not believe it is that it is so simple and matter-of-fact.

The rule also states that the leader should spend 100 percent of his or her time with the undecided group and the change-friendly group and ignore the resisters. Resisters cause 80 to 90 percent of the problems and make the most noise. They will try to poison the other 70 percent if you give them a platform. Let's face it. Some unfortunates just will not change, so spend no time with them. (These squeaky wheels should get no oil!)

I know it is sometimes hard to just forget about 30 percent of the people in your group, but talking to them is a great waste of time. They are generally not in favor of any change. Spend your time, money, and effort on the 70 percent who are willing to change or are neutral. Don't argue with those who are not on your side. They will enjoy the spotlight and cause problems for you. Failing to ignore the resisters is a major error many make, and this costs those people a lot of unnecessary stress, misery and failure.

Some resisters will come around and go with the majority in time, but most won't. It's just not your job to worry about the resisting 30 percent. Ignore them.

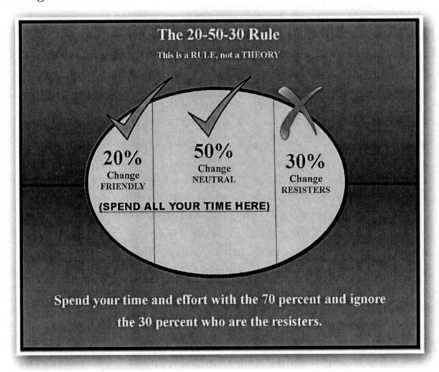

However, not everyone is equal when it comes to resisting change or embracing it. This rule tells you the truth about the group as a whole. Never forget about the individuals in the 70 percent. They do not all think the same. They do not all have the same talents. They do not all have the same attitude. They are not all natural leaders. These four examples are just the tip of the iceberg when discussing the differences you find in every group.

In some change-management movements I have been involved in, sometimes the leaders forget that each group is made up of individuals. They try to treat everyone as an equal. Do not fall into that trap when working with any group. Every group is made up of individuals—not clones. When leading a group, you need to discover what each individual is good at and exploit his or her positives. You should lead your 70 percent by seeing your group as what it is: a group of individuals agreeing with your plan or premise in time. All this might seem obvious, but it's amazing how those in charge (who are otherwise solid leaders) make the mistake of treating each person the same. As a leader, be sure you live in the real world.

Some individuals have more influence than others. Here is what I mean. The more powerful the resisting person (employee), in terms of job title, position, and longevity, the more success he or she will have in resisting. Less-well-positioned employees might resist collectively through an organization, such as a union or a clique.

How do these individuals resist? Resistance to change appears in actions such as verbal criticism, nitpicking details, failure to adapt, snide comments, sarcastic remarks, missed meetings, failed commitments, interminable arguments, lack of all verbal support, and outright sabotage. There are many other kinds of resistance. Those mentioned are some of the most common. The 30 percent who are the resisters might resist as a collective group. The vast majority of them will more often resist as individuals in that group.

The 20-50-30 Rule has worked for tens of thousands of people. Your life and your company will improve and become less stressful if you use it. It works every time. Sometimes the hardest part of the 20-50-30 Rule is to believe it is true. If you can believe this rule on a consistent basis, you will succeed more and have a lot less stress in your life. If you are a leader, the 20-50-30 Rule will improve your ability to lead. The benefits are hard to overstate.

In the next chapter we will go into more detail about the resistance to change and how to handle it successfully. You will learn what only a few ever have the chance to know.

CHAPTER 3

Resistance to Change

*Faced with the choice between changing
one's mind and proving that there is
no need to do so, almost everyone gets busy on the proof.*
—John Kenneth Galbraith

Resisting change is normal. We all resist change to some degree. Why? Is it because we know that change can evoke painful emotions? Whether the change is positive or negative, we know some pain is coming, and it is only natural that we try to avoid it. We cannot change the emotions we have; neither can we alter our natural resistance to change. What we can do is influence our reactions to the emotions that all change will cause.

Some say that change isn't the problem—resistance to change is. I would not go that far, but this does point out that resistance is a huge problem. Resistance can be dangerous to our families, our employees, and the groups we belong to. Do not underestimate what resistance can do to a change-management plan—or a person's life.

Here's a story about Jed and his first camping trip. As soon as Jed pitched his tent, he went for a hike in the woods. In about twenty minutes, he rushed back into camp. He was bleeding, limping, and in a lot of pain. "What happened?" asked a fellow camper.

"A black snake chased me!" cried the frightened Jed.

The camper laughed and made fun of Jed. "A black snake isn't dangerous. It has no poison. It is not dangerous."

"Listen," Jed said, and then he groaned. "If it can make you jump off a fifty-foot cliff, it is dangerous!"

It is true that a black snake is not poisonous, so it cannot hurt you that way. However, the snake did cause Jed a lot of pain and hurt. Change can be like that in a way. The actual change is not what can cause you so much hurt and pain. It might be the stress, anxiety, or fear that you experience anticipating the coming change. Resistance to change can cause you a lot of pain.

Resistance is the opposition offered by one thing to another. That is simple enough to understand. *Webster's Dictionary* says that resistance means "the refusal to accept or comply with something; the attempt to prevent something by action or argument." The opposite of resistance is cooperation and acceptance.

Most of us have a good idea of what resistance is from our own experiences. Resistance can be a positive or negative action, but when we resist positive change, it is negative. Resistance can be frustrating and exhausting for the resister. We often resist things we do not understand. We might have deep-seated fears about change, and that can cause resistance. In dealing with a group or a team, we must address resistance to change before the change takes place. The leader must have the trust of the group or team. You can build trust by being very honest and truthful about what is going to happen. Tell the truth very well. There is some truth in the saying, "The truth will set you free."

It is important to accent as many positive-reinforcement behaviors as possible in the face of the pending change. Tell people all the positives about the coming change. For some, point out what can happen if they do not change. Sometimes you must do both. Talking about the negatives that will happen if the change does not occur can open some eyes. This might reduce the resistance to the change. If such legitimate concerns are not addressed quickly and fully, a morale problem could arise. Left dangling, these concerns will come back to haunt management. Being completely open, accessible, and willing to answer all questions fully goes a long way toward eliminating employee concerns. Management's attitude toward such questions will make a big difference. It is not just up to the employees to endorse the coming change. It is management's job to put the employees at ease as much as possible through management's attitude, willingness to tell the truth fully, and willingness to change. The leaders and change agents must be good examples of what these leaders want the group to be and do.

The information about resisting change can also be helpful when you are going through personal change. In a one-on-one tough talk with yourself, tell yourself how you might be guilty of resisting and why. By understanding why you resist change, you will become better equipped to be more flexible. Change is constant, and I often find it necessary to have a long and sometimes tense conversation with myself about what I believe but have not put into practice. Most of the time, I am a pretty good listener. There are times when I directly or indirectly continue to resist. While I'm describing this situation about me, the word "stubborn" keeps coming to mind. All of us resist change to some degree. It is our human nature to resist pain. It is the degree of resistance to change that is important. Simply because you experience some amount of resistance does not mean that you go automatically in the resistance column. It is the degree of resistance that should make the final call.

When using the 20-50-30 Rule, you begin to classify each person in the group into one of the three categories, but please remember that it is the degree of resistance that counts.

As a quick review, here are eleven reasons we will resist change on a regular basis.

Reasons We
Resist Change

The Thought of Fear
Lack of Trust
Bad Habits
Belief that Change is Unnecessary
Self-interest
Happiness with Status Quo
Loss of Control
Poor Communication from Management
Reluctance to Learn New Skills
Constant Feeling of Loss
Lack of Job Security

Resistance to change is always going to be with us. There are many reasons why resistance is always a part of any planned or unplanned change. Expect resistance. The feelings that the emotions of change cause are at the root of all resistance to change. These feelings always occur. The key is how to control them. The good news is that this is 100 percent doable.

In dealing with people you are going to find folks who are just difficult to work with for many reasons. For some reason, there seem to be more of this kind of person in the resistance group. Next we will talk about how to handle difficult people.

CHAPTER 4

How to Deal with Difficult People

*Those who expect moments of change to be comfortable and
free of conflict have not learned their history.*
—Joan Wallach Scott

The 20-50-30 Rule is an important and widely accepted principle that we have already discussed. You already know that, for the most part, it is best to ignore resisters, with few exceptions. Leave them alone.

What are some of the exceptions to leaving them alone? A senior member of management would be one. You must deal with this person before you begin or implement any type of change plan. Another exception might be someone who could have a political impact on your change plan. For example, let's say a member of your staff is also a state senator who could be of value in making a state law that allows your change to go forward. Don't ignore that person. Maybe your boss has made it clear that his or her son is to be on the change-management team. Obviously, you must get the son on board with your idea. In all these cases—and others I'm sure you've thought of—you must bring these folks into the fold before the change process begins. How do you deal with these people if they are part of the resistance? Here is a list of ways to bring a person into the fold. Keep in mind these are very rare exceptions to the rule of ignoring the resisters.

1. Start your indoctrination and teaching before the change process is even started.
2. Conduct these teachings on a one-to-one basis.
3. Hold these meetings or sessions in private and on the resister's home turf. If that is not possible, have them at some neutral location.
4. Have someone of equal or higher position (rank) than the one you are trying to convince do the persuading or be a part of the small group that has been chosen to talk to that person.
5. Never let this person feel as if he or she is on trial. Always use a friendly, low-key voice and a conversational tone. Never be confrontational. Anything that even hints at an argument or rebuttal will not succeed. If you put him or her on the defensive, you will have lost.
6. Show respect for the other person's point of view. If you can find points you do agree on, bring them up, and discuss them briefly. Be careful not to say anything the other person can use against you later in the conversation or in the overall process.
7. Show the person what could or will happen if the pending plan does not take place. Rely on facts—not hunches.
8. Be sure your tone of voice is upbeat and pleasant. Voice tone is 38 percent of all communication. Your tone can make or break you when you are making a point.
9. Listen to all the resister says. Before you leave his or her presence, you should have addressed all of his or her points. Let the resister know that you appreciate his or her candor and will be addressing many of the mentioned concerns in detail during later meetings. Often, the concerns brought up during this initial meeting end up determining your agenda for the next several meetings if they become necessary. It is rare that this type of resister will be convinced by meeting only one time.
10. Ask the person many questions about his or her objections. These should be learning (leading) questions. For example: "Can you tell me more about that?" or "Let me see if this is what you are saying." They could also be questions about objections you do not understand.

11. If, after a time, the resister refuses to accept the change, first make sure the person absolutely refuses to see the positive side of the pending change-management plan. When you are certain you have hit a brick wall, your only recourse is to go back to top management, tell them that the person cannot see the positive side of the plan, and ask for his or her removal from the change-management team. If management refuses, you should advise top management not to try to set up or implement the plan. The change-management plan should not be started until this situation is resolved.

12. Realize that changing someone's mind is not easy. It is not necessarily fun or exciting, and you probably have a lot riding on your success or failure.

13. A cardinal rule is never, never, never show anger. "Anger is an acid that can do more harm to the vessel in which it is stored than to anything on which it is poured," (Mark Twain). You must not let yourself get angry. If you do get angry, never let the other party see or feel it. Fake it. Become a thespian. Do whatever it takes. The best solution is to not get angry.

14. Make sure you have good posture and are open with your motions. For example, do not cross your arms. Body language is 55 percent of all communication.

15. Speak in the language of the hearer (listener). The language level depends on the other person's education level, experience in the company, knowledge, and so on.

16. Give the other person your undivided attention. Do not look through your notes or out the window when he or she is talking. This is not a small thing. If he or she thinks you are not listening, let your body language show the person that is not the case. When the other person is talking, do the correct thing and listen. Use your open body language to prove you are listening. Show the resister you are paying attention by nodding your head from time to time or making some other positive gesture. I wish I had listened better to my mother's words. Here are just a few

tongue-in-cheek things I remember I learned from her the few times I listened to her:

a. Mother taught me about *logic*:
   "Because I said so, that's why."

b. Mother taught me about *irony*:
   "Keep crying, and I'll give you something to cry about."

c. Mother taught me about *religion*:
   "You better pray that will come out of the carpet."

d. Mother taught me about *time travel*:
   "If you don't straighten up, I'm going to send you into the middle of next week."

e. Mother taught me about *contortionism*:
   "Will you look at the dirt on the back of your neck?"
   And finally...

f. Mother taught me about the science of *osmosis*:
   "Shut your mouth and eat your supper."

17. Make sure your words do not come back to bite you. The words you use are only 7 percent of communication; however, they can help make the right (or wrong) impression. Be aware that if conversations are being recorded, your words and voice tone will be the only record. Your body language will not play a part in a recorded audio communication. So be careful with your words. Similarly, your voice tone will not help if your words are put in writing. If that is part of the plan, you will be communicating by words only.

Dealing with difficult people is something we all go through, both at work and at home. Let me tell you from personal experience that crow does not taste good. Your job is to improve the performance of the largest number of team members. It is not your job to humiliate and embarrass them. Your job is to make a difficult person come over to your way to thinking. Good common sense can make a big difference. This goes along with your own patience and understanding. The goal should be better performance—not punishment. Keep in mind that the 20-50-30

Rule should apply in almost all cases. A smile and a pleasant attitude will go a long way in helping you communicate your point of view.

In order to succeed you must have a pleasant and positive attitude. In the next chapter we discuss the importance of just that. It is all about attitude.

CHAPTER 5

Attitude and Change

Attitude is a little thing that makes a big difference.
—WINSTON CHURCHILL

The correct attitude is a requirement when a change agent is planning for or implementing change. The correct attitude is a must for success. But what is attitude, anyway? Attitude is a feeling or way of thinking that affects a person's behavior.

It has been said that up to 96 percent of a person's or company's success is based on attitude. A positive attitude is clearly necessary to lead, and this is particularly true when leading change. It is important to know that your thoughts have a direct, solid impact on your attitude and, therefore, on both your professional and personal lives. You are what you think. Thoughts that you think regularly end up becoming beliefs. The Golden Rule from the Bible is a great example: "Do unto others as you would have them do unto you," (Matt. 7:12).

Your attitude affects your ability to make correct decisions in life. Thomas Edison said he tried over 10,000 different filaments before finding one that would do the job for his lightbulb. Edison was proud of the fact that he never gave up. Where would we be if he had stopped trying after 9,999 attempts? Most of us give up far too quickly. Staying strong and not giving up is based on overall attitude.

A scientific experiment mirrored how most of us act when we face failure over and over. Scientists placed a shark along with some baitfish in a holding tank. The shark immediately ate the baitfish. Then the researchers placed a strong, heavy sheet of clear fiberglass between the shark and the baitfish. The shark did as expected; it went after the baitfish in a frenzy. Instead of getting a free lunch, though, it slammed into the clear fiberglass wall. It did this about every two or three minutes (to no avail). Time after time, the shark hit the fiberglass wall. An hour into the experiment, the shark gave up.

Over many days, the experiment was repeated with the same shark. Each time, the shark became less and less aggressive and made fewer attempts to attack the baitfish; the clear wall stopped it each time. The shark eventually got so tired of hitting the wall and failing that it finally would not attack the baitfish at all. The shark just gave up. Then the researchers removed the fiberglass wall so that the baitfish were an easy meal. The shark still did not attack. It had been conditioned to the idea of the barrier. The shark gave up when there was no longer any barrier. We all can learn from this experiment. After experiencing failure after failure while trying to accomplish goals, most of us give up and stop trying. After repeated setbacks, we see walls between us and our goals. We assume that because we have failed repeatedly, there is a barrier—where none might exist. Winston Churchill said in a commencement address to a boys' school, "Never, never, never, never give up!" In fact, this was his entire speech that day. After he said those now-famous words, he thanked the crowd and sat down to a standing ovation. Most barriers that we think are there might not exist at all or can be conquered. We should never let anyone or anything keep us from trying again. Memorize Churchill's speech.

An experiment I took part in while I attended the University of Tennessee went like this. I was taking a physiology course in my junior year. The professor offered extra credit if anyone in the class would be a subject for one of his studies. I signed up. Here was what happened. The professor brought me into an empty room. He placed me in the center of that room and grabbed a shoebox of small pieces of paper. There were hundreds of separate pieces of paper in that shoebox, and he dumped the paper on my head. The small pieces of paper went everywhere. Some stuck in my hair, and the majority landed on the floor around me. He then instructed me to pick up every piece of paper. It took about twenty minutes to pick up all of them. Then the professor placed all the pieces of paper I had just picked up back in the shoebox. He placed me back in the middle of the room, dumped the shoebox full of the paper on my head again, and told me to pick up the pieces. I was annoyed, but I did what he asked a second time. The effort took another twenty minutes. He did the exact same thing to me three more times. The last time, I almost told him no, but I thought better of that. I was exasperated and mad, but I picked up the pieces of paper for the fifth time.

After the fifth time, he asked me how I felt. I sure did enjoy telling him my thoughts. I felt better when I finished. As I told him how mad I was, I became even more upset. It ended up being a very unpleasant experience for me. However, I learned a lot about myself by being a participant in his study. Here are some things I learned:

1. Your circumstances can have a great effect on your attitude.
2. When you see no reason to have to do something, it can quickly change your attitude toward the task and the person who asked you to do that task.
3. Having to do something you dislike repeatedly can cause you stress and can change your attitude toward the person who asked you to do it. I disliked doing the task, but I disliked the person who made me do the task even more—for a short period.
4. Sometimes the purpose of having to do a task I dislike might not be worth the effort. In my case, it was for extra credit on my grade. I wanted the extra credit, so I did what he asked five times. However, it pretty much ruined my attitude for the entire day. One event during the day can affect your attitude for a long time after the event has happened.

How many other lessons can you come up with?

Let me state the obvious. Outside forces and situations can change a person's attitude. It is up to the individual to have the discipline to compensate for these outside forces. If you are not careful, often outside forces can have a negative effect on your attitude toward the task or whatever the outside force is at the time. Maybe not quite so obvious is the change in attitude that can also occur toward things and people who are not associated with the outside force. Your attitude is your number-one asset. Be careful that outside situations or people are not able to control your attitude. Stay in control.

Charles Swindoll said the following about attitude.

"The longer I live, the more I realize the impact of attitude on my life. Attitude to me is more important than facts. It is more important than the past, than education, than money, than circumstances, than failures, than success, than what other people think or say or do. Only you should be in control of your attitude. It is more important than appearance, a gift, or a skill. It can make or break a company…a church…a home. The remarkable thing is we have a choice every day. We cannot change our past…we cannot change the fact that people will act in a certain way. We cannot change the inevitable. The only thing we can do is play our own game well. I am convinced that life is 10 percent what happens to me and 90 percent how I react to it. And so it is with you…we are in charge of our attitudes. Attitude is the most important ingredient in our success as a person. Always stay in control of your attitude."

Here are some interesting thoughts that others have about attitude:

A positive attitude may not solve all your problems, but it will annoy enough people to make it worth the effort.
—HERM ALBRIGHT

The only disability in life is a bad attitude.
—SCOTT HAMILTON

If you aren't fired with enthusiasm, you will be fired with enthusiasm.
—VINCE LOMBARDI

There are no menial jobs, only menial attitudes.
—WILLIAM J. BENNETT

To be wronged is nothing unless you continue to remember it.
—CONFUCIUS

*The only difference between a good day
and a bad day is your attitude.*
—DENNIS S. BROWN

*When written in Chinese, the word crisis is
composed of two characters. One represents danger,
and the other represents opportunity.*
—JOHN F. KENNEDY

*A happy person is not a person in a certain
set of circumstances, but rather a person
with a certain set of attitudes.*
—HUGH DOWNS

Positive anything is better than negative thinking.
—ELBERT HUBBARD

*Things turn out best for the people who make
the best out of the way things turn out.*
—ART LINKLATER

It isn't our position but our disposition which makes us happy.
—ANONYMOUS

Excellence is not a skill. It is an attitude.
—RALPH MARSTON

If you want to change your life, change your mind.
—ANONYMOUS

Believe you can, and you're halfway there.
—THEODORE ROOSEVELT

What lies behind us and what lies before us are
tiny matters compared to what lies within us.
—RALPH WALDO EMERSON

These great men and women say clearly what I believe to be true about attitude. The importance of a positive attitude is hard to overstate. A great salesperson knows that if a competitor's product is equal to his or her company's product—with the cost of delivery and the product and all other facts about the competition's product being the same— the salesperson with the best attitude will almost always make the sale. The best attitude, in some cases, will trump even a lower price from the competition. I have seen this happen in my company more than once. A great attitude is a super advantage to the person who possesses it. Why attitude is not more often discussed in company sales meetings is beyond me. A great attitude will take you a long way up the ladder fast—and keep you there.

Let me tell you a true story about myself. I hope it will show you how far some people will go not to change their attitudes. One of my goals here is to communicate how to embrace positive change and not resist it. Here is an example of my resistance to change because of a bad attitude and what happened because of it.

Some forty years ago, I was doing very well. I had a great family, a good business position, and the opportunity for all of it to grow and prosper. I had made some excellent connections in the political world. Life was good. According to society's scorecard, I was living the American dream. I was doing well. However, the real story was that I was miserable. No matter how many toys I bought myself or how many business successes came my way, I always felt empty, and I could not figure out why. After all, look at all I had.

By some measures, I was doing very well indeed. If all that was true, why was I not happy? Somehow, I knew there had to be more to life than the misery I was living in. However, instead of facing my unhappiness head-on and making appropriate changes, I followed the path of most self-centered people: the path of least resistance. I followed what society said was best for me, and I paid the price. Ego and arrogance are strong motivators, and we must learn to not listen to them.

At this time in my life, I was studying change academically but failed to see the obvious connection. I continued doing the same things and expected my happiness to improve. It did not. Some of you might recognize that what I was doing is one definition of insanity. My life was a disaster. I was very miserable and ran to alcohol to kill the pain. Rather than change, I decided to work on one of the symptoms of the problem—the pain—rather than the cause of the problem. I readily admit that I knew better, but pride was in charge, and I followed it to more misery.

Constantly, a small voice was saying, "Ralph, this is not it." This small voice quietly and constantly told me to change, but I would not. Change and give up the so-called good life? No way. I again and again refused to change my attitude or anything else. I tried to drown the quiet, small voice in alcohol. More and more alcohol was my solution to the misery. No matter how much I drank, though, the voice was still there. I would not change. Things got worse and worse.

In the business world, things were actually getting better—thanks to my partners. My personal and spiritual life, however, was at absolute zero. This misery went on for over twenty years. My life was a disaster because I would not consider changing.

At one point, I turned to religion to give me some relief from the mental pain and sorrow. Note, I said religion; I did not say a relationship with a higher power. The religion I practiced was one of legalism and performance. I had no relationships with anything. I became a hypocrite and an almost perfect Pharisee and performer.

During my "religious time," I seldom missed church. The worse the weather, the more determined I was to be there. In my arrogance and legalism, I was sure that attending church would make a difference. There is nothing wrong with attending the church of your choice. However, I was there for all the wrong reasons. I had again deceived myself into thinking that I could perform my way to a happier life. Things got worse.

My attempts at such trickery did not work. This was no surprise to anyone but me. I, of course, did not fool God or the people of that church. In time, it became clear even to me that performance and legalism were not going to make things better. In my deceived brain, it was clear that God, as I knew Him at that time, was against me. I left the church.

Things got even worse. Not only was I miserable inside my soul, but now things were not going well in my family or business life. My family life was a wreck. I began to miss work because of my addiction to alcohol.

I could not and would not be a good father or husband. I generally ignored my family. I could not and would not run my business correctly because of my addiction to alcohol. It was clear to me that I had to do something. I thought a lot about what to do. I decided to take the coward's way and drink more alcohol, and I did just that. I was out of control. I was insane.

Again, one definition of insanity is continuing to do the same thing but expecting a different result. Based on my actions, I was a poster child for insanity. Here is more proof.

Things got worse because I would not consider changing. One afternoon, I was in a drunken stupor. I went to my closet and loaded a double-barreled, twenty-gauge shotgun. With that loaded shotgun in my hand, I sat down in a chair and took off my left shoe and sock. At point-blank range, I aimed that shotgun at my heart and pulled the trigger with my toe. I tried to commit suicide, and it almost worked. When I pulled the trigger, though, my aim was a little off. Instead of hitting my heart, I blew my midsection apart. It was a serious injury, and I was not expected to live. I was rushed to the hospital forty miles away and was on the operating table for over six hours. I was in intensive care for a week, and then I was moved into a regular room for two weeks.

One afternoon at the hospital, a group of five or six doctors came into my room, and the lead doctor said, "Mr. Masengill, you are a medical miracle."

"What do you mean?" I asked.

He said, "First of all, the number-eight shell you used was old and contained rust and dirt. There was a one hundred percent chance of infection. You do not have an infection. We have double-checked, and you are infection free. Ralph, that is amazing."

He continued, "You were shot at point-blank range with a twenty-gauge, number-eight shell. Ralph, do you know how powerful the force is behind that kind of shell? Are you aware of the kind of pattern a number-eight shell makes at point-blank range? Are you aware of how many pellets are in a number-eight shell? Mr. Masengill, not a single pellet hit any vital organ. Not one pellet hit either kidney. None hit your spine or your spinal cord. They all completely missed your liver, spleen, and stomach. One hundred percent of the shot landed only in your intestinal tract. We did some calculations, and we estimated that even if we welded that shotgun to a steel tripod and froze your body in solid ice, we do not believe it would be possible to miss all your organs with a point-blank, twenty-gauge, number-eight shell. We believe there would be only a million-to-one probability of success. The truth is, most of us do not believe that kind of shot is possible. You did it without trying. It is truly amazing. If there are such things as miracles, this is one of them."

When I came home from the hospital, I was still ungrateful for my life being spared. I continued to drink for another two months. At that point, I began to listen to that quiet, consistent voice, and I entered an alcohol-treatment program. That is where I connected with my spiritual side and developed my new attitude.

All this took place over forty years ago. From that day on, I have been totally alcohol free, and I began to enjoy a life of peace, joy, and true success. I have even lost my compulsion to drink alcohol.

I am a truly blessed person, and I am very grateful for all the things that have happened in my life, both good and bad. What a wonderful thing it is to live in love, peace, and joy. Again, I am grateful for a second chance. After years working with others who have been addicted to alcohol as I was, I know how rare a second chance truly is in today's world, and I am now profoundly grateful.

I got a second chance because I finally took a calculated risk and embraced positive change. I know from personal experience what can happen if you do not (or do) embrace positive change. I learned the hard way that it is necessary to take calculated risks and embrace positive change with a great attitude. You can learn from my many mistakes.

Today, I have a wonderful family with a beautiful wife, four grown children, seven grandchildren, one cat we call Bandit, and two dogs, Beau and Charlie. My business successes have been substantial and far better than before the fall.

Let me close this chapter by mentioning just some of the important points and reasons that a good attitude is important. A good attitude is more than important. It is mandatory for real success. We all need to make sure our attitudes are positive for our own health and well-being. We need to remember that a great attitude will make success easier for us. Keep in mind that outside forces, sometimes ones that we have no control over, can and will alter our attitudes if we are not on guard. A good attitude is your number-one asset. Be sure you give it the value it deserves. Protect your positive attitude at all costs. A solid attitude and change management must come together to be successful. I suggest you take a moment before you move on to chapter 6 to review this chapter. It is that important. People with great attitudes are like sweet-smelling, colorful flowers: everybody likes to be around them.

True success requires a solid, positive attitude and a willingness to go through the pain of change on a regular basis. Next we will discuss positive and negative change. Positive change is the cornerstone of lasting success.

CHAPTER 6

Positive and Negative Change

*It may be hard for an egg to turn into a bird: it would be a jolly
sight harder for it to learn to fly while remaining an egg. We are
like eggs at present. And you cannot go on indefinitely being
just an ordinary, decent egg. We must be hatched or go bad.*

— C. S. LEWIS

The pain of change is something we all have endured. We react
to change the same way and feel the same about it whether it is
positive or negative. However, the influence of negative change is
different. Unfortunately, it has two and a half times the effect or power
over us that positive change has in the very short run.

Negative Change

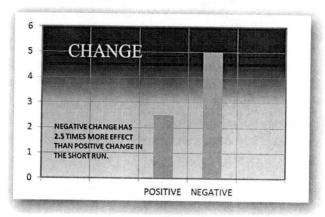

This is a big deal. In the change movement, I have found over the years that this data has not been given enough attention. It makes sense that if we have more than twice the reaction to negative change as we do to positive change, we need to know our enemy, negative change. Some of the reactions we can have when we experience negative change are well-known. Having said these truths about negative change, I will repeat the most important one. Be aware that the reaction caused by negative change only works in the extreme short run. Here is a short list of some of the most significant reactions to negative change:

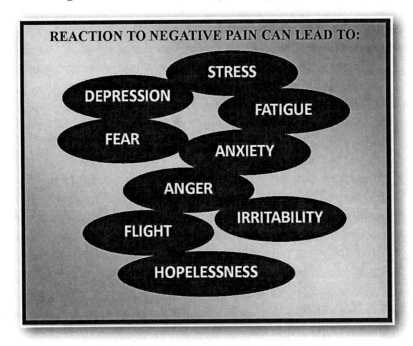

REACTION TO NEGATIVE PAIN CAN LEAD TO:
STRESS
DEPRESSION
FATIGUE
FEAR
ANXIETY
ANGER
IRRITABILITY
FLIGHT
HOPELESSNESS

There are many other reactions that can happen. This depends on the individual and the situation. This short list is for illustrative purposes only. I'll discuss some of these possible reactions in more detail later.

When you are aware of the various reactions that negative pain can cause, you are better able to cope with change. First, know that you will have a reaction to it. Second, know the types of feelings the emotions of negative change can cause. You can use this knowledge to go through the experience with a less severe reaction than some of those on the example list. You might not be able to stop these emotions, but you can control your feelings about them. You cannot stop the reaction you have to negative pain; so you need to learn to recognize the symptoms for what they are. Your reactive feelings can become a bigger problem than the pain of negative change itself. Your reactions to the feelings these emotions from negative pain cause can lead to even more serious problems. For example, deep depression can be a much bigger problem than the loss you endure through experiencing the actual negative change by itself. In fact, this is normally the case with negative pain.

Knowing how to react to the pain of change can make a significant positive difference in your overall personal health and happiness. When you can limit your reaction (feelings) to the emotion that negative change causes, be sure to give yourself credit. Pat yourself on the back. Give it a try. I bet you will like the results. Pain from positive or negative change is treated the same. The effect of pain from negative change is two and a half times more powerful than that of positive change, but only in the short run.

Pain from negative change comes in many forms. There are times when you must go through the pain of negative change to correct a negative situation. As I've mentioned, you might need to go through negative change to make sure that positive change happens or continues. Sometimes, negative change occurs just because it is a part of life. Here are a couple business-related examples:

Close a branch office. You have a branch office that is not pulling its weight, and your board has decided to close it. You give your employees three options: they can move to another office in a city forty miles away, take early retirement, or be laid off with severance packages. You are not only changing all the employees' situations; your action also impacts everyone in an employee's immediate family. This kind of negative change must be handled with skill and understanding. Knowing how those affected will react to this change is important for you, your team, and your company. However, closing the branch is necessary for the greater good of the company and all the other employees who are not directly affected.

Let an employee go. Have you ever heard of a post turtle? Being labeled one is not a positive thing—at least not in the part of Tennessee where I live. Here is the story of the post turtle.

An old farmer says, "Well, you know, some people are like post turtles." Not being familiar with the term, a friend asks him what a post turtle is. The old farmer replies, "When you're driving down a country road and you come across a fence post with a turtle balanced on top, you're seeing a post turtle." The old farmer sees the puzzled look on his friend's face, so he continues. "You know that turtle didn't get up there by itself. It doesn't belong up there. It doesn't know what to do while it's up there. Now, that is a post turtle." I do wonder what kind of person put it up there to begin with.

Can you think of any post turtles in your business? I can. I hope none are in your company or in your family. Post turtles, as you might expect, are not well thought of by other team members. However, the person who put the post turtle in his or her job might end up being the one who loses the most respect, prestige, and power.

Other team members hold leaders accountable for job promotions and the positions they fill. Appointing the wrong person could end up being a lose-lose situation for both you and your company. The first thing you must do is determine if you have any post turtles. All good leaders know the capabilities of new team members based on résumés, references, personal knowledge, and so on. Leaders know this before hiring or promoting anyone. With all that information, however, HR managers or the person making the promotion can still make mistakes. It's a good idea to go back every six months or so and check on all team members you have brought into the group or have promoted. A leader's job does not end with the appointment or promotion. Monitor your actions. Give your appointments some time; give them a good chance to work. Then decide what to do about the action you have taken.

A leader sometimes fails to recognize that placing the wrong person in a position can result in a real threat to his or her own ability to lead. Team members follow those they respect. If you have added or promoted someone who is not working out, it could affect your personal reputation with the team and the performance of the team or group.

It is important to take appropriate action when you discover a post turtle. This action is an example of going through negative change in order to make positive change happen.

What if your business has to downsize, and you have to reduce staff? You will be dealing with serious negative change. All change must be taken seriously, and all change will have an impact on you and your staff, but it is always important to keep in mind that negative change has two and a half times the impact of positive change in the short run. Again, sometimes it is necessary to go through negative change to allow positive change to take place.

Unexpected negative change happens more often than most of us imagine, and it can result in a shock to the emotions. How you react to this kind of negative change can affect your happiness and your position in the business marketplace. Here are a few examples of the kinds of changes you might face:

- You are told of the sudden death of a friend or family member.
- The customer says no to your major sales presentation.
- Your main competitor introduces a brand-new product.
- You discover that your competition has lowered prices below your markup.
- You come home from vacation and discover your water pipes have broken. There is two inches of water throughout your home.
- You suddenly become sick and must enter the hospital and miss work.

Positive Change

If we have to go through the pain of change, we would much prefer positive change all the time. Negative change, though, is often necessary to bring about a positive change in the long run.

For example, having a child means a woman must go through the negative pain of childbirth. After the birth, the couple must endure midnight feedings, a crying baby, endless diaper changes, and so on. However, most couples find that these kinds of negative changes are worth going through to reach their noble goal of having offspring.

Another example: I have a client who planned to go through much negative change to meet the needs of his changing customer base and allow his company to grow and prosper. We worked together and planned for more than a year for the various kinds of negative change he and his employees would have to go through to reach the positive change we were seeking. Some of the things we put in place were letting go of 25 percent of the workforce. A 20 percent cut in individual benefit packages and cutting paid vacations by one week. It was not easy; in fact, it was difficult to go through the pain of the negative change. Today, though, he and the vast majority of his employees would agree that all the negative change was worthwhile to see growth continue. It brought the owner and the other stockholders more profit and secured a solid job base for all the employees.

Change of any kind creates some form of anxiety. Stress, fear, and anger are three other common examples, but there are many more. What you feel depends on the type of change and the makeup of your personality. The important thing is to know how these emotions will affect you, your team, or both. You must plan for these emotions. You cannot stop them from happening, but you should react to them correctly. Knowing that change will alter everyone's emotional state goes a long way toward lessening the effects of the emotions brought on by change. The reactions we have to both positive and negative change are basically the same. Both affect your emotions. We generate feelings about these emotions. The good news is we can control the feelings caused by the emotions that we have about this change. Your job is to be ready when these feelings manifest themselves.

The mistake is to ignore these feelings. Based on the best research available, change will absolutely affect your happiness and your ability to win. Take change seriously, and you will prosper. Of course, you can control the feelings you have from the emotions that all change generates. You cannot control the emotions change will bring. Change is a part of life. If the change is positive, in most cases, you would not want to change it if you could. Negative change causes the same pain as positive change. You can, however, control how you react (your feelings) to both positive and negative change.

Let us look at two specific reactions to the change. Please take a close look at the quote that begins the next chapter.

CHAPTER 7

Fear and Anxiety Caused by Change

Change can be scary, but you know what's scarier?
Allowing fear to stop you from growing,
evolving, and progressing.
—MANDY HALE

hange creates a feeling of loss, which in turn creates some form of fear or anxiety or both. When people go through change, whether positive or negative, they suffer from the pain of fear or anxiety. Let's explore how fear and anxiety affect our emotions.

First, let's explore fear. What is fear? From a number of dictionary entries and my own research, I've put together the following description: fear is an emotion induced by a real or perceived threat that causes a change in brain and organ function and ultimately a change in behavior, such as running away, hiding, or freezing in the face of traumatic events. This is the fight-or-flight response. Fear is a distressing emotion aroused by impending danger, evil, pain, and so on, whether the threat is real or imagined; it is the feeling or condition of being afraid. Synonyms for fear include foreboding, apprehension, consternation, dismay, dread, horror, trepidation, qualms, terror, fright, and panic. Fear can be helpful in some cases—but almost never when caused by impending change.

Most of us have experienced a fair share of fear in our lives and have a good idea of what fear is and how it makes us feel. What we might not be aware of are the best ways to overcome unwanted fear. What are some good ways to approach this painful emotion? Fear causes stress in all of us, and remember that stress can be a killer. We need to take fear for what it is: a serious, unwanted, painful feeling that can, however, sometimes keep us out of trouble. We are going to discuss the kind of fear that hinders us rather than the kind of fear that keeps us away from troubling situations or things. In other words, we're going to discuss fear we do not want in our lives.

You have probably heard it said that if you face your fears, you will have less fear. That is not necessarily true. When you face your fears, you might gain a deeper understanding of the fear you are experiencing, but the fear does not go away simply because you have recognized and confronted it. Perhaps you find that the fear is not as huge as you thought. On the other hand, it might be larger than you thought. Please do not misunderstand what I am saying. Yes, we do need to face our fears. Until we are willing to face our fears, little, if anything, will happen to dissipate them. Face a fear if you want to conquer it. Face a fear if you want to see it eventually go away. There is no other way. Many have tried other ways, but I bet half the ranch that they did not work. You must face your fear. At the same time, eliminating the fear does not necessarily make the emotion of the fear go away.

Here are two extreme examples of fear that I have gone through. The first is a true story about an armed jailbreak that happened in my hometown.

Let me set the scene. The jailbreak was at about two o'clock in the afternoon. At about four-thirty of the same afternoon, law officers from several counties, the city police, and the Tennessee Highway Patrol surrounded a duplex apartment about three blocks away from the jail. They were positive they had seen the escaped prisoner head directly for that duplex.

Law enforcement tried for about an hour to get the armed prisoner to give himself up, but he never came out. Then the police began to doubt he was in the duplex. They rushed the door and knocked it down, but they waited for an additional fifteen minutes to give the prisoner one last chance to come out peacefully if he was in fact in the duplex. As a bonded deputy sheriff, I was behind a great big shrub with a Tennessee Highway patrolperson. I was just looking around and waiting for the fifteen minutes to pass. I don't know why, but I decided to check my weapon, a twelve-gauge pump shotgun. When I did, I glanced inside the large bush we were standing behind for protection, and I saw a .38 pistol aimed at both of us.

When I saw the escaped prisoner, I backed away from the bush and asked the Tennessee trooper to join me. He moved back a little. That's when I stepped in front of the bush, pointed the shotgun into it, and told the escaped prisoner, who now had his back to me, that I would shoot him if he moved. He turned just enough to see my twelve-gauge aimed at his head. He dropped the .38 and put his hands in the air. The prisoner was taken back to jail, and my day of excitement was over. We had been hiding behind the very bush that armed escapee had been hiding in. The Tennessee trooper and I both considered ourselves very fortunate that the criminal had not panicked and shot both of us.

By then it was after six o'clock, and I took the rest of the day off. I went home and tried to pour myself a glass of tea, but I was so nervous that I spilled it all over the table. I had faced the fear and won. The cause of the fear was gone. However, I was still reacting to the fear that no longer existed. The experts tell us that a reaction from a fear that has been eliminated can last for years in some people.

(For the record, back in the seventies in our county, ordinary citizens could become unpaid bonded deputy sheriffs. The sheriff had made me one as an additional reward for handling his first successful bid for office. That was why I could be part of the hunt for the escaped prisoner.)

Here is the second extreme example. This is another true story that happened to me and a friend.

During the time of Fidel Castro's reign, a pastor friend of mine and I went on a "mission trip" to Cuba. At that time, Cuba was a military state with Castro as the dictator, and the country had no diplomatic relations with the United States. You will understand the words "mission trip" being in quotes as this story progresses. The pastor and I were there for about a week. After we had been there four days, the Cuban army arrested us both at our hotel pool area, and we were taken to Cuban army headquarters for interrogation. We were taken under guard to a small room in the basement of army headquarters. The room had no windows and was dimly lit. As we entered the sparsely furnished room, I could see a desk and an army captain sitting behind the desk. He was surrounded by three uniformed guards with pistols on their hips and rifles over their shoulders. In addition, there were two other people dressed in civilian clothes to the left side of the desk, and they kept staring at us for some reason. It was clear they were trying to intimidate us, and from my point of view, it was working. I was scared. The captain was in his fancy uniform, and he told us to sit down in front of his heavy wooden desk. We did so quickly. He told us we had committed grave crimes against the people of Cuba and its government.

When the captain said that to us, I became very scared—and with good reason. I had Cuban friends who had spent years in Cuban prisons on trumped-up charges. He pointed to two typed legal documents positioned in front of us on his otherwise empty desktop. He looked us in the eye and told us that it would go better for us if we signed the two typed confessions we had before us. The confessions were in Spanish with an English translation on a separate piece of paper to the side of the confessions. We refused to sign, and he was not happy. The captain and the two people dressed in civilian clothes then tried to convince us to sign the confessions for some time. We would not sign. After what seemed like hours and hours, the captain said for us to go directly to our hotel. He also said we could no longer drive a car on Cuban streets. He ordered us to be at the airport at 9:00 a.m. The Cuban government was about to deport us.

We left gladly. Through other friends in Cuba, we were able to contact the bishop of Cuba, and he worked a real miracle. When we arrived at the airport, an army colonel met us, and he began processing us through customs. When we started that process, the colonel had the airport shut down. This was a large airport, and until we were processed and out of the country, nothing else at the airport was allowed to operate. We were not deported; however, we did leave Cuba that morning and were told we could never come back. We were grateful and relieved to be on our way back to the United States. When we talked to the bishop of Cuba after we arrived safely home in the United States, he told us how he had handled our problem.

It just so happened that the head of the Catholic Church—yes, I am talking about the pope—was coming to Cuba about six weeks after we got in all this trouble. The bishop told the Cuban government in Havana that if they did not treat us well and let us depart on our own, the pope would cancel his visit. Whether that was true, I cannot say. I do know that we were freed. I am very grateful to the bishop and the church for intervening on our behalf. The pope's visit was well-known by all the people of Cuba and the world. The Cuban press had been talking about the pope's visit for months, because it was going to give much prestige to Fidel Castro and Cuba. If the pope had not come, it would have been a huge disgrace for Castro. The plan worked, and we were allowed to leave on our own.

Now, here's the rest of the story about our trip. The facts are that we were not necessarily on a "mission trip." We were in Cuba to set up an escape for one of the bishop's pastors and his wife. My pastor friend was carrying a great deal of money for that purpose, and that was, of course, a criminal offense in Cuba. About three months after our visit to Cuba, they both did escape to the United States. Both were liberated and now live in America. For the record, they are both university graduates and have good jobs here in America. I cannot tell you where they are located other than to say they both made it to our shore and freedom.

The two people dressed in civilian clothes in that room in the basement of the army headquarters were spies. They had been following us during our visit to Cuba. They had even broken into our hotel rooms and looked for incriminating evidence. I cannot tell you how I know this information. Some of the people involved in this rescue are still in Cuba and need to be protected.

Yes, it was a super learning experience. Was I scared? You bet I was. I was probably the most scared I'd ever been in my life. I know from first-hand experience what fear, stress, and insecurity are all about and how debilitating they can be to anyone. I would not trade anything for what I learned about myself from this experience.

Experiencing fear and suffering through an experience can indeed teach a lot about how a person will act when in danger—supposed or real. Going through fear can teach a lot. This has to be one of the toughest ways to educate yourself about this subject. Do not ever put yourself in fear just to learn more about it.

Ways to Fight Fear and Win

Overcoming fear is a learned response. If you do not teach yourself to overcome fear using your own mind or with the help of others, you will not be successful. The first goal in conquering your fear is to admit to the fears you have. You should make a list of all the fears you can recognize. Try hard to list as many as possible. We fear some things more than others. Be sure to list even your minor fears as part of this exercise.

Any fear causes a fight-or-flight reaction. You must choose to fight. This might take some discipline to do correctly. Once that is done, you are ready to move on to conquering your fears.

Seventeen Facts to Help Beat the Pain of Unwanted Fear

1. The more often you purposely face one of your fears, the easier it is to face the next one.

2. Take one step at a time. Facing a fear is the first step. If you do not first face your fears, you will not be able to eliminate them at a later stage of the process. Eliminating your flight response to as many fears as possible is the goal. Remember, a fear that has been eliminated is not necessarily a fear that will not cause you problems.

3. Writing down your fears is step two in the process of eventually breaking the hold a fear has on you and eliminating it.

4. Trust me when I say that facing your fears is hard. You will, however, find it more than worth the effort.

5. It is not unusual to become so familiar with living in fear that you are afraid your attempt to eliminate it is a mistake or a negative experience. You might believe it is normal to have all this fear and even try to convince yourself that most people have this much fear. It is not normal to have a lot of fears. Becoming comfortable with the familiar (living with great fear) is one way you stay in fear's bondage.

6. Be as specific as you can when listing your fears. The details count. Being specific will give you a better picture of your fears

and the level of bondage those fears create in your life. It is important to pinpoint exactly what you fear. You must be able to describe accurately what you are afraid of if you are to eventually conquer it. In some cases, this might require professional help. When you list your fears on paper, you might need just a word or two to express some of them; for others, you might need a paragraph or more. Keep it real. Write down only the reality of the fear. Don't write what your imagination wants to tell you it is. Again, only the facts will do. This can be a real stress reliever.

7. An attitude of gratitude is a great way to counter your fear. When your fear arises, instead of focusing on it, discipline yourself to focus on something you are truly grateful for. This can help conquer the pain you are experiencing.

8. If perception is reality, then change your perception, and you can change your outlook on reality. When you fear something, replace it with a different perception. When you work on this technique, it can become almost second nature. Use the control you have over your mind to control your fear. Gather all the facts, and use them to change your perception.

9. Fear is not only painful in the moment; it can also be detrimental to your health. All fear causes some form of stress (along with other things), and you now know that stress is a killer. You must take your fears seriously.

10. Ask yourself why you have a particular fear. Look for the root of it. I have found that my fears are often unfounded and make no logical sense. That discovery has allowed me to move on to the next fear and my goal of gaining peace, happiness, and joy. Ask yourself the simple question of why you have that fear. See if you can figure out why the fear exists. You can control your fear. Is fear in charge, or are you? You can be in charge of your fear and your life. Why not go for it?

11. When it comes to facing your fears, your imagination can be your enemy. Imagination is a wonderful thing to have—except when it exaggerates the negative. Many times, a fear feels larger than it really is. Be careful of the exaggeration that your imagination dreams up about some of your fears. See the fear as it is. Don't

see it as your imagination presents it. Do a reality check about your fear. This will save you a lot of pain. Do not go to war with imagination. Keep it in check, and deal only with the facts.

12. Sometimes you cannot get rid of a fear without professional help. This is nothing to be ashamed about. Fear can, without much effort, make you ill. Most of the time, people do not realize how much they might need professional assistance. Always keep this option open. If you are committed to a life free from the effects of unwanted fear, get help if you need it. It is always worth the effort. As Nike says, "Just Do It."

13. Self-talk is a good way to make correct decisions about your fears. Be sure to keep your conversations with yourself positive. Address the emotions that fear is causing one at a time.

14. Keeping a positive attitude will help you deal with fear. Use your discipline to stay positive about the effects of the fear on your attitude. This is often difficult, but it is a choice you have to make. Choose to walk on the sunny side of the street. It will bring you closer to your goal of peace, happiness, and joy.

15. The food you eat affects your mood and your ability to resist the effects of fear. Remind yourself that fear is an emotion. Be careful what you put in your body. Remember the old accounting phrase: garbage in, garbage out. Respect your body, and it will serve you well.

16. When you have submitted to unwanted fear for whatever reason, you must admit that fear has control. You need to admit you are in bondage to your fear or fears. Your goal is to reverse the process. The freedom you will experience when you have conquered your unwanted fear is wonderful and life changing.

17. Changing your approach to fear actually causes some fear. It is time to gain control of your fear and begin to live the good life. Instead of worrying about and reacting to the negative emotion of unwanted fear, grab life by the horns. Make a difference in this world and in your life. One of the opposites of fear is contentment. I like the sound of that word.

Contentment is the feeling of being well satisfied. Other words that might help define "contented" include pleased, fulfilled, and happy. It can also be a state of serenity, gladness, pleasure, and feeling at ease. One of the opposites of contentment is conflict or fear. Working from some dictionary definitions, I've put together this definition: to conflict means to come into collision or disagreement with or be contradictory or in opposition to. A conflict can be a clash or a state of war—declared or not. Fear can cause us to experience all these states of mind within ourselves and about ourselves. When we are in conflict with ourselves, we tend to experience a lot of anger.

Fear can zap your courage. We all have a good idea of what courage is inside ourselves. Courage is the ability to face danger, difficulty, fear, uncertainty, or pain without being overcome by it. Synonyms for this positive emotion are valor, gallantry, bravery, and guts. Courage is not an absence of fear; it is an overcoming of that fear or going around it.

Fear can cause you not to take calculated risks. Fear can cause you to think irrationally. There are risks, and then there are calculated risks. Risk is the danger that injury (physical or otherwise), damage, or loss will occur. Calculated risk is much different. It is a well-studied risk that research indicates offers a good chance for success. In other words, it is when a person, based on study and research, decides that taking the risk is worthwhile. Yes, there is a risk that you will not be successful, but based on your research and your well-thought-out opinion, there is a better-than-average chance of being successful. You just don't know exactly what size the better-than-average odds are.

Fear can keep you from becoming all that you want to be in this life. We all have goals (things we would like to accomplish). Fear can keep you from believing in yourself and stop you from planning for success in the present and the future.

Fear can cause you to think incorrectly about everything in your life, and may not be directly related to the fears you have. If you fear taking an exam, that can also cause you to do poorly on a paper you must write for an English class. Many people do not understand how great an impact fear can have on their lives and the people they're around. Even the very courageous among us have fears they must regularly face. The difference is that they possess the solid willingness to face their fears and eliminate them quickly. They understand that fear causes stress and can lead to bad decisions. These brave folks are aware that fear makes them less effective in everything they do. People of courage know the dangers of uncontrolled or unattended fear. Your fears will not go away on their own. You must pursue them aggressively to succeed at your highest level. All fear cannot be eliminated. However, all fear can be controlled.

Ways to Overcome Fear

Fear is a motivator, but it is a painful one. You might be motivated out of fear to finish a project by the deadline. You might fear you have not studied enough for an exam you are about to take. Fear is more likely to create chaos and stagnation than any other kind of motivation. It is possible to fear so much that your system will not function. If you do nothing to eliminate the fear, that can cause more fear. It is true that fear can feed on itself. We need to overcome unwanted fear.

It is not easy to overcome unwanted fear, but when you do, it is rewarding and beneficial to you for the rest of your life. What is the best defense against this negative emotion? A saying in military circles is this: "The best and fastest path to victory is to know your enemy like the back of your hand." That advice will serve you well when you are learning to understand unwanted fear. Here are a couple of my favorite quotes about fear:

> *I must not fear. Fear is the mind killer. Fear is the little death that brings total obliteration. I will face my fear. I will permit it to pass over me and through me. And when it has gone past, I will turn the inner eye to see its path. Where the fear has gone, there will be nothing. Only I will remain.*
> —FRANK HERBERT

> *Fear is inevitable. I have to accept that, but I cannot allow it to paralyze me.*
> —ISABELLE ALLENDE

I wonder how many restless and nearly sleepless nights I have spent in mortal fear of something either real or imagined. Here are thirteen thoughts to put in your arsenal of fear-fighting weapons:

1. The real secret to fighting fear is to understand it and the emotions it causes.
2. Knowledge is the best defense and offense for beating fear.
3. When thinking about fear, your imagination can be your enemy.
4. You must be brutally frank about what you fear.
5. It is common to doubt yourself when facing fear. Doubt is often a form of fear. Set it aside, and face one specific fear. When you've eliminated it or have it under control, go on to another fear.
6. Accent the positives in your life, and set the negatives and supposed negatives aside. This might be harder at first than you think, but do it anyway.
7. Take a moment to check your OK factor. You have fears in your life, but look around. Are you OK right now? The chances are excellent that what you fear is not attacking you right now, at this very moment. Try to relax; you're not in battle at present. You will feel a little more at ease after checking your OK factor. Do it several times a day to bring yourself back to reality about your fears.
8. To set your mind at ease, take five to thirty minutes a day to meditate. If you prefer, pray. They are both great ways to start or end your day.
9. Remember what President Roosevelt said: "The only thing we have to fear is fear itself." The fear of fear can keep you in bondage and make your life miserable and unhealthy. Fear is a form of anxiety as well as a short-term motivator. The fear of fear might not be rational, but the emotions it can evoke are very real and need to be addressed.
10. Face your fears; do not ignore them. Ignoring them will not make them go away. In fact, it can make things worse. It is running away. Hiding your fear from yourself is a mistake. Do not play the ostrich game. Suck it up, and attack the fears that are attacking you.

11. It is important that you have a plan of attack for confronting your fears. Use what you have learned about fear in this and other books to formulate your plan. Write down your plan on paper. Remember, failing to plan is planning to fail.
12. Often we refuse to even admit that we are experiencing fear. To deal with it, you must admit to yourself that you have a fear or fears. You must acknowledge your fears.
13. You might not be able to eliminate all your fears, but you can control your reactions (feelings) to the emotions that fear can bring.

Do not let fate be your answer to ending your battle with fear. Fate can be defined as circumstances that befall someone or something over time. I believe that allowing fate to take its course means deciding to do nothing to change the circumstances in your life. Don't expect fate to solve your problems. Develop your plan, and then work it to conquer fear or control it. Take control of the fear or fears in your life, and stop conning yourself by letting fate be in charge. If you stick with your battle against fear, you will succeed, and you will never regret all the hard work that it sometimes takes to beat or control this nemesis. The wonderful freedom you can feel is almost overwhelming when you win. Do not let fear paralyze you. Do the work required. Liberate yourself.

Conquering fear requires serious decision-making. You must decide who is in charge of your future and what influences, emotions, and feelings you will allow your mind to process. This decision can change your life. Here is a story that can help explain what I mean:

One fine day, a grandfather was telling a story to his grandson. The grandfather said, "Did you know that there is a big battle going on between two black bears inside you? One bear is evil, and that bear is always doing bad things. The other bear is good, and this bear is always doing the right things."

The grandson quickly asked, "Which bear wins?"

The grandfather replied, "The one you feed."

We have control. All of us face fear in our lives; we must choose whether we feed that fear or feed peace, joy, and happiness. The truth about fear is that we should be in charge of how much of it we let into our lives. Conquering fear is hard; there is nothing easy about it. The rewards, however, are huge.

A Quick Look at Anxiety

The terms "fear" and "anxiety" are often used interchangeably, but they are not the same.

Anxiety is a feeling of worry, nervousness, or unease. It is typically about an imminent event or something with an uncertain future outcome. Ridding yourself of some types of anxiety often requires the help of a medical professional.

Fear is a response to physical and emotional danger. This can be real or imagined. It is an unpleasant emotion caused by the belief that someone or something is dangerous, likely to cause pain, or a threat.

As you can see, the two are similar but not the same. I am not a trained medical professional, so I don't feel qualified to go any further with the definition of anxiety. However, to help differentiate it from fear, I offer these twelve signs that you might be suffering from anxiety:

1. You often think irrationally.
2. You experience mental and physical pain for no apparent reason.
3. You seem to be depressed more than normal.
4. You have negative thoughts without a reason.
5. You do not know why you feel anxious.
6. You have stomach cramps that have no physical cause.
7. You increasingly experience nausea.
8. You worry about many things.
9. You feel nervous most of the time for no identifiable reason.
10. You are a perfectionist.
11. You have problems sleeping.
12. You doubt your ability to succeed.

I have listed the signs and symptoms of anxiety that I am most familiar with, but there are others. Suffering from one or more of these problems does not necessarily mean you are experiencing more anxiety than normal. But if many of them apply, you might want to visit a medical professional about your situation. It is always better to be safe than sorry.

Fear and anxiety have kept many geniuses from making their marks on the world. Once you know how fear and anxiety operate in the human mind, you can control them or eliminate them.

Facing fear and anxiety is not easy. It requires us to take a risk every time we face them. In the next chapter is about how to take a calculated risk with confidence.

CHAPTER 8

Risk of Change or Supposed Security

The pessimist sees difficulty in every opportunity.
The optimist sees the opportunity in every difficulty.
—WINSTON CHURCHILL

One reason we resist change is that we often prefer the supposed security of known misery to the anticipated misery of the unfamiliar. We feel there is some risk to change, and there always is. Many people choose not to take the calculated risks that change requires for many reasons, some of which we've already discussed. Some people would rather stay in their ruts of known misery or supposed security. Others prefer to roll the dice, and others live in denial.

It is true that you will not skid in a rut. However, you have no control over where a rut in the road takes you. If you resist change, you lose your freedom. Are you in a rut?

Many good people refuse to accept the calculated risk and uncertainty of change. They force themselves to live in self-imposed, stagnant prisons of their own making. I call these ruts. When it comes to change, you really have only two choices. One is to embrace change with gusto, and the second is to deny that changes need or must be made. We must learn to take calculated risks to conquer change and win.

Risk is a chance of loss or a chance that something will go wrong. Risk is the probability of being harmed or harming others. Risk can be very painful. Why take risks? For one thing, there is no change without risk, and change is the only way to advance or improve. Without risk-taking, no real positive change is possible. That said, when dealing with change, we want to be sure that we take only calculated risks.

One of the greatest risks you can take is to avoid all risk. Think about it. Without risk, there is no progress in your business or personal life. Risk is as necessary as breathing if you are to have true peace and joy in life and success in business. A calculated risk is a good thing. A different definition from the one given earlier of a calculated risk is a well-thought-out action with established goals and a clear, specific deadline with both a time and a date.

Let me go on a tangent for a moment. It is important that deadlines be clear and unambiguous. Give a person a time—not just a date—to be crystal clear. There was a time when I knew almost nothing about deadlines. I once asked a staff member to prepare a report by June 1. I expected the report on my desk by 9:00 a.m. that day, but the staff member saw the deadline as the end of that working day. I was disappointed, and the staff member made a bad impression on me. However, the staff member had done nothing wrong. I had made the mistake of not being clear. When I got the report at 5:00 sharp, I considered it eight hours late. The staff member, however, was proud she had been on time. Avoid unpleasant uncertainties and confusion by setting very clear deadlines. What if I had scheduled time to read the report at 10:00 a.m. in order to present it to the board of directors at noon? With a time-and-date deadline, you can eliminate a lot of confusion, stress, and, like in the example above, even possible chaos. You owe it to your staff and yourself to be clear about what you expect. I feel better. Now, let's get back to the discussion of risk and risk-taking.

Let's talk about the chicken-or-egg problem with change and the risks involved. Where should you start? Let's look at an example. You are the CEO of a business whose employee expenses are too high for the employees' level of productivity. Your solution is to bring in more tools for the staff members so they can work faster. Since the staff should be more productive, you plan to cut personnel by 20 percent.

How do you proceed? Do you test how much the new tools have increased each employee's efficiency and quality of output and lay off those with the lowest 20 percent of test scores? Do you lay off the 20 percent of employees with the lowest seniority and then bring in the new tools? There are pros and cons to either method. There are many other ways you can also consider.

The leader might choose a method based on calculating the risks of each. Here, they are about equal. The important thing is to accept that there is always risk. The risk of not changing—not stopping the financial bleeding—is the real problem in this example.

Calculated Risk versus Risk

Everything we do involves some form of risk. We have all taken well-thought-out, calculated risks and failed. Don't ever let that stop you from thinking outside the box. Even when I have analyzed the risk correctly and done everything right in my preparation for taking the risk, I must still push myself to make the right decision sometimes. This is especially true if the risk appears substantial. However, indecision caused by fear or other factors can cause you to wait too long to implement the decision. When you have the facts, make a decision promptly.

All the risk we voluntarily assume should be calculated risk. Many people use the term "risk" as shorthand for calculated risk. You improve your odds of success if you research a risk you are facing. However, sometimes you must take on a risk quickly. Regardless of how quickly you must act, there are certain steps you should always take—even if you have to ask for a deadline extension. Here are those steps.

1. Make sure you understand why you are considering taking the calculated risk. Have a clear picture of what you want to happen when you take the risk. What is the goal?
2. List all the pros and cons you can think of. Decide if the amount of risk you are considering is worth the reward.
3. All negatives and all positives do not carry the same weight. Give the proper weight to each.
4. Write down your goals.
5. Write a plan for accomplishing your goals. An old saying goes, "Until you commit your goals to paper, you have intentions that are seeds without soil." You must write down everything about

your goals and your detailed plan to reach them. Do not take shortcuts.

6. Don't overestimate the possibility of failure. Most of us do; we're just made that way. Sometimes you are your own worst enemy. Know all the negatives that can occur if the calculated risk fails. In some cases, there might be negatives even if you are successful after taking the calculated risk.

7. Never bet the ranch. It is important for you to be able to afford the loss if your plan fails. Yes, you can learn from your failures, but it sure is painful and expensive.

8. Assess your ability to recover from the negative outcome if the project fails. Analyze how much you can expect to lose if the project is a bust. It is sometimes difficult to get otherwise well-meaning managers and CEOs to do this. They often refuse to even consider failure and its cost to them or the company. Those who do not consider the possibility of failure are not only foolish but poor leaders.

9. Now estimate the risk of not taking on the calculated risk. The risk you are measuring might be to yourself, your company, or both. Sticking to the status quo might be the easy route, but it can many times lead to potential disaster. Can you maintain the status quo if nothing is done?

10. What are the facts of the current situation and your educated assessments of the future if you stay where you are in the current business or personal cycle? Be honest and open when assessing the status quo. Take into account all the work and effort that implementing the change will require in addition to your regular duties. Be aware of your own personal bias against or for the proposed risk and all risk in general. Work hard to keep bias out of your decision-making process. This does not mean you should not consider your opinion.

11. Check and recheck the source for every fact you use. Using bad data can lead to making a bad decision—no matter how hard you work and plan. Taking a calculated risk can be one of the smartest things you've ever done...or the dumbest. If you deal with old or inaccurate information, you cannot make a good risk decision.

12. Time your decision well. Even the best decisions can be timed badly. If you wait too long or not long enough, your situation might be adversely affected.
13. Never make your decision on a whim.
14. Plan for errors. No plan is perfect, but no implementation of a plan is perfect either. If you do not plan for errors, you add to the number you make by at least one. You must be ready when a hiccup or something bigger occurs.

When you use these points as a framework for your risk-taking plan, not only will your effort be more likely to succeed, but you will have a high level of confidence in your decision once you make it. Calculated risk-taking should not be a gamble. You enhance your probability for success by doing your research and having your tentative change-management plan in place before you start the change process.

We all take risks every day. Are they calculated risks, or do we sometimes roll the dice and hope for the best? The former is acting on opportunity; the latter is acting out of ignorance. I admit that in my younger days, I did more rolling of the dice than I want to talk about. Taking calculated risks can lead to success, but most other risk—some call it gambling—usually leads to failure.

Those who try to avoid all risk tend to drive calculated risk-takers up the wall. First of all, it cannot be done. There is always risk because there is always change taking place. Change is constant. Consider the professional bureaucrat. Out of fear of making a mistake (or a wave), his or her favorite words are "no" and "not yet." Calculated risk-taking is a good thing. It's where most jobs come from in the United States.

Many successful people have things to say about risk-taking. According to Warren Buffett, "Risk comes from not knowing what you're doing." Author and lecturer Earl Nightingale said, "You can measure opportunity with the same yardstick that measures the risk involved. They go together."

Is security the opposite of risk? Some say it is, but I believe those people are in error. Here is what Helen Keller had to say about security: "Security is mostly a superstition. It does not exist in nature, nor do the children of men as a whole experience it. Avoiding danger is no safer in the long run than outright exposure. Life is either a daring adventure or nothing." Former President Eisenhower said, "One can find outright security only in a prison. In order to be absolutely secure, you must give up your individual freedoms." I believe total security is a myth. Here are some more quotes from wise people who believe in taking calculated risks:

To be alive at all involves some risk.
—HAROLD MACMILLAN

It seems to be a law of nature, inflexible and inexorable, that those who will not risk cannot win.
—JOHN PAUL JONES

Only those who will risk going too far can possibly find out how far one can go.
—T. S. ELIOT

There came a time when the risk to remain tight in the bud was more painful than the risk it took to blossom.
—ANAIS NIN

One doesn't discover new lands without consenting to lose sight of the shore for a very long time.
—ANDRÉ GIDE

It is better to have enough ideas for some of them to be wrong than to be always right by having no ideas at all.
—EDWARD DE BONO

Don't be afraid to go out on a limb. That's where the fruit is.
—H. JACKSON BROWNE

You won't skid only if you stay in a rut.
—KIN HUBBARD

Those who try to do something and fail are infinitely
better than those who try nothing and succeed.
—LLOYD JONES

It's not so much that we're afraid of change or so in love
with the old ways, but it's that place in between that we
fear...It's like being between trapezes. It's Linus when his
blanket is in the dryer. There's nothing to hold on to.
—MARILYN FERGUSON

I am always doing that which I cannot do,
in order that I may learn how to do it.
—PABLO PICASSO

Decision is a risk rooted in the courage of being free.
—PAUL TILLICH

Only those who dare to fail greatly can ever achieve greatly.
—ROBERT F. KENNEDY

In this chapter, we are not talking about gambling. We are talking about taking a calculated risk. The differences between the two are huge. Gambling is basically rolling the dice; you are willing to let fate or the odds be in charge. In most gambling situations, you are unlikely to win, and that is through no fault of your own. After all, the house must make a profit to stay in business, and the odds are in their favor. I believe that risk is a form of gambling. Calculated risk is not.

With calculated risk, though, you are accountable for your actions. In gambling, the odds have control. To be successful in life or business, you must learn to take calculated risk regularly. Some people see both kinds of risk as a form of excitement; others see it as a living hell. Taking calculated risk is a learned process that can lead you to more success.

Taking risk of any kind can cause some form of stress. That is the subject of the next chapter.

CHAPTER 9

Managing the Stress Caused by Change

It is not necessary to change. Survival is not mandatory.
—W. EDWARDS DEMING

Being overwhelmed by change is normal and will happen to some degree to all of us. After all, you have your regular duties, and now you must add change to the list of emotions you must endure. Many times, change makes a paradigm shift necessary and takes you out of your comfort zone.

A personal or business change can cause you to experience some fear. How you handle that fear affects the amount of stress you will endure. You can lessen—or, in some rare cases, even eliminate—the amount of stress you experience. You can be in charge of how much stress you must endure to accomplish the planned change.

Limiting your stress is not easy, but it is well worth the effort. First, the change you are about to go through is easier to manage if it is not forced. For the record, you manage forced change and voluntary change in the same way. You can experience change in a better way if you get involved in making it happen. If management has not asked for your help, consider volunteering. Go the extra mile. This will show your boss that you are a team player, and it will give you a feeling of being a part of the change—not just one of the staff members required to change. It can give you a sense of control. In personnel change, you will automatically be involved.

If you have a lot of tension and get a stress headache, do what it says on the aspirin bottle's label. It states clearly, "Take two as needed, and keep away from children." I have four grown children and seven grand-children. I love them very much, but there have been short times when I did not like them much.

To make change more palatable, tell yourself it is a mind game. You have control of your mind; thus, you can control the feelings that the emotions of change bring. You cannot eliminate the feelings, but you can control the attitude you have about those feelings. You can control your reactions to the feelings you are going to have. All this can go a long way toward helping you control your stress and achieve a better life in general.

Stress is a killer. Do not let stress overtake you. You can fight back. Stress is serious stuff that will affect your health, mood, energy level, at-titude, and income. Here is my favorite story about stress:

Back in the thirteenth century, two monks were walking down a dirt road. During their journey, they came upon an old woman who was wait-ing to get out of her sedan chair. Recent rains had left large puddles in the road. They were so wide and deep that the woman could not cross the road without soiling her spotless silken robes. There she stood. She was on the wrong side of the road, and she looked very impatient and upset. She was yelling at her attendants. The attendants could not help because of the large packages and luggage they were carrying for her. They could not put the packages and luggage down because of the wet, muddy ground.

The younger monk noticed the woman but did nothing to help as he walked by her. The older monk quickly picked her up, put her on his back, and carried her to the other side of the road by walking through those big, deep puddles. The woman did not acknowledge the monk's kind deed. Instead, she snarled at him and pushed him out of her way.

The two monks continued on their journey. After a couple hours, the younger monk said to the older one, "That woman back there was rude and hateful, but you picked her up, put her on your back, and car-ried her across those mud puddles to the other side of the road. She did not even thank you for your efforts. In fact, she rebuffed you for your kind deed!"

The older monk replied, "I set that woman down hours ago. Why are you still carrying her?"

This story hits home with me. Like the younger monk, I often carry around stress. This is true even when I know it is not necessary. We never stop learning, and I hope someday to master the technique of the older monk. I have been working on my problem for more than thirty years, and things are getting better, but I am still not there. This makes it clear to me that knowing and understanding are not enough. I must believe. I must practice what I know to be true.

Preventing the pressure of change from turning into stress is something we all need to address. Does pressure always cause stress? No, it does not. The key is making sure that the pressure remains pressure and does not lead to the killer stress. Some pressure is actually good for us. Yes, you should strive to meet your deadlines, but doing that does not have to move you into stress.

The words "stress" and "pressure" are not synonymous. They are not the same thing, but some see little difference between the two and use them interchangeably.

Pressure is something that affects thoughts and behavior in a powerful way. It's usually in the form of several outside influences working together persuasively. You can feel the pressure of someone trying to get you to do a task, or you can apply pressure to someone else by asking him or her to complete a task by a certain time-and-date deadline.

On the other hand, stress is something that causes someone to experience mental, emotional, or physical pain through anxiety, overwork, fear, and so on. Stress can cause high blood pressure, depression, and similar maladies. Pressure is often a good thing. It helps us get things done in a timely manner. Nothing good, however, can come from the effects of stress in our lives. As we are aware, stress can ruin health, happiness, peace, and joy. It is important to not confuse stress and pressure. If you are under pressure, you are not necessarily under stress. Pressure can be your friend; stress is never a friend.

Here is a quick, humorous demonstration of pressure—or is it stress? An elderly man was on the operating table awaiting surgery to be performed by his son, a renowned surgeon. Just before they put him under, he asked to speak to his son: "Don't be nervous, son; do your best, and just remember, if it doesn't go well, if something happens to me...your mother is going to come and live with you and your wife." I believe it is stress of the highest order.

I often demonstrate what stress is in my lectures by raising a small glass of water to the audience and asking, "How heavy is this glass of water?" The answers called out generally range from twenty grams to five hundred grams. Then I say that the absolute weight is not the major factor. What's important is how long it is held up—how long I carry it with me. If it is held for a minute with my arms out in front of me, it's not a problem. If I hold it for an hour, there will be an ache in my arm. If I hold it for a day, you'll have to call an ambulance for me. In each case, the glass is the same weight, but the longer it is held, the heavier it becomes. This is how stress works. Let go of stress. It is a killer.

If you carry a burden around all the time, it becomes increasingly heavier. Eventually, you won't be able to carry on with your life. As with the glass of water, you need to put that burden down for a while and rest before holding it again. When you're refreshed, you can carry on with your goal. So before you leave work tonight, put your burdens down. Don't carry them home with you; you can pick them up again tomorrow. The burdens you carry around may be pressure today but can turn into stress if not handled properly.

Let's lighten up this very serious subject with some fun. Here are some ways to deal with stress:

- Just accept that some days you're the pigeon, and some days you're the statue.
- Keep your words soft and sweet—just in case you have to eat them.
- Drive carefully. It's not only a car that can be recalled by its maker.
- If you can't be kind, at least have the decency to be vague.
- If you lend someone twenty dollars and never see that person again, it was probably worth it.
- Never put both feet in your mouth at the same time. You won't have a leg to stand on.
- Nobody cares if you can't dance well. Just get up and do it.
- It is the early worm that gets eaten by the bird, —sleep late.

- The second mouse gets the cheese.
- When everything's coming your way, you're in the wrong lane.
- Birthdays are good for you. The more you have, the longer you live.
- You might be only one person in the world, but you might also be the world to one person.
- Some mistakes are too much fun to make only once.
- A truly happy person is one who can enjoy the scenery on a detour.

Here is one last example. A friend told me this story many years ago:

A man picks up a girl who is hitchhiking. Suddenly, she faints in the car, and he takes her to the hospital. Now, that's pressure. At the hospital, though, they say she is pregnant and congratulate the driver on his impending fatherhood. He says he is not the father, but the girl says he is.

This is getting somewhat stressful! The man requests a DNA test to prove he is not the father. It does prove he is not the father. The doctor further says the man can't be the father because he's infertile—probably since birth. He's relieved but upset at the news of the infertility. On the way back, the message sinks in, and he thinks about his five kids at home. Now that is stress.

The moral of the story is that sometimes when you solve one situation with the facts, these facts can present an even bigger situation you must address.

Sometimes the stress keeps coming and coming. I hope these examples and stories help you understand what stress is all about. You'll experience less fear and anxiety from stress when you understand how it works and how to minimize it.

The more we understand something, the better we can combat it. Understanding stress can be a stress reliever by itself. The same is true for change. The more we understand change, the better we can react to the feelings that the emotions of change cause. Eliminate all the unnecessary stress you can. Do this whenever you can. Change can cause stress. Stress hurts your creativity and your body. Pressure, on the other hand, can be a positive force in your life and business. Please take a minute for a quick look at the very blunt and perhaps in-your-face box below about stress.

A Truth about Too Much Stress

STRESS

IS A

KILLER

Practice what you know. Let me close this chapter by leaving you with some quotes about this killer called stress:

No one can get inner peace by pouncing on it.
—HARRY FOSDICK

*Stress is an ignorant state. It believes
that everything is an emergency.*
—NATALIE GOLDBERG

*I try to take one day at a time, but sometimes
several days attack me at once.*
—JENNIFER YANE

*A crust eaten in peace is better than a
banquet partaken in anxiety.*
—AESOP

*If your teeth are clenched and your fists are
clenched, your life-span is probably clenched.*
—TERRI GUILLEMETS

*Tension is who you think you should
be. Relaxation is who you are.*
—CHINESE PROVERB

*There cannot be a stressful crisis next
week. My schedule is already full.*
—HENRY KISSINGER

*When I look back on all these worries, I remember the story
of the old man who said on his deathbed that he had a lot
of trouble in his life, most of which had never happened.*
—WINSTON CHURCHILL

In the middle of difficulty lies opportunity.
—ALBERT EINSTEIN

He who smiles rather than rages is always the stronger.
—JAPANESE PROVERB

*If people concentrated on the really important things
in life, there'd be a shortage of fishing poles.*
—DOUG LARSON

CHAPTER 10

Decision-Making During Change

*It does not take much strength to do
things, but it requires a great
deal of strength to decide what to do.*
—ELBERT HUBBARD

Good decision-making is vital; we all understand that. The change plan you are involved with will fail or succeed based on the quality of the decisions everyone makes. If I thought there was a stronger word than "vital," I would use it. Each person's success or failure is determined by the quality of the decisions he or she makes.

Solid decision-making is about choices. In decision-making, you are in charge. Decision-making is choosing between available options. A set of facts might lead to several options, and your job is to choose the best one. Decision-making always causes change.

One fall evening many years ago, my wife and I were in bed, and I whispered in her ear my feelings about her. She smiled and said, "When I'm eighty and I think about my life and what it was like to be young, I hope that I can remember this moment." A few seconds later, she closed her eyes and went to sleep. I stayed awake for a while and thought about the time we had spent together and all the choices in our lives that had made this moment possible. Each choice requires some form of change. The choices you make today affect both the present and future of your life and those of the people around you. Take the time to make your choices wisely.

The choices we make are integral parts of change and change management. These choices are often taken lightly. They should not be. Mark Twain put it this way: "The difference between the right word and the almost right word is the difference between lightning and the lightning bug." We must be determined to make the very best decisions and choices possible. Making no decision is, in itself, a decision. We make decisions regularly; the key is to choose the decision-making process rather than allow it to be made through inaction. I am often surprised to hear someone say, "I have decided not to make a decision." Well, in fact, he or she has just made a decision. After all, what does the word "decide" mean? Don't be fooled by those who procrastinate or those who do not have the courage to make timely decisions. They might convince themselves that no decisions were made, but we should understand that decisions were in fact made. They have chosen to let indecision make the decisions rather than take the bull by the horns and choose what the situations demand (based on the accurate data at hand). Either way, decisions have been made.

The reason we make a decision should be examined. "Am I biased toward the wrong reason?" and "Why am I leaning this way?" are questions we should ask ourselves in decision-making. All of us have a personal agenda, and we should boldly admit that truth. Your decisions should be made based on the facts and not on personal preferences. In the business world, there are few exceptions to this rule. Mark Twain demonstrates a personal agenda this way: "Adam was but human—this explains it all. He did not want the apple for the apple's sake, he wanted it only because it was forbidden. The mistake was in not forbidding the serpent; then he would have eaten the serpent."

I belong to a nonprofit organization that is losing members. At times in the past, we had regular attendance of about 125 at our meetings. Today, regular attendance is down to about fifty. The group is considering a marketing plan to increase membership. First, though, the nonprofit must go through all the bureaucratic steps before any plan can even be presented—let alone put into practice. So far, that has taken about eight months, and it looks as if it could be another six months before anything will be considered. Don't get me wrong. These are great people who have made decisions. They do not see them as decisions, but decisions have been made. For the present, the organization has chosen to do nothing to correct the problem directly by saying data is still being gathered. This is often an excuse given to continue not making a decision and delay. The group has indeed made a decision. I am hoping in time the group will agree to a complete marketing plan. In the meantime, group attendance continues to decline.

In decision-making, it is important to verify the data you are basing your decision on. Always check your facts. If you are listening to several sources of advice, make sure the sources (people or groups) have the credentials to give you their opinions on the subject. One of my pet peeves is that often a decision will be made in a committee meeting based on a vote of the committee members. The number of yeas and the number of nays make the decision. This often happens in volunteer meetings or meetings serving a nonprofit. More than likely, some of those voting do not have enough experience or knowledge to give well-founded, grounded opinions. However, their votes carry the same force and effect as votes from the members of the committee who are informed on the subject. If that happens, you do not have good decisions in most cases, if ever. For example, I would make a terrible member of a committee on women's fashion. Be careful whom you seek advice and council from in decision-making. That does not mean you do not want to get advice and opinions from many. Just give weight to those people who have the knowledge and experience to give you informed advice on your subject. The loudest, squeaking wheel might not be qualified to give you an informed opinion.

That does not mean that committees should not vote when deciding issues. What is the solution, then? Make sure everyone on the committee is qualified through experience, knowledge, or both. Don't get me wrong; we need and must have committees. The key to a great committee is always the members. Great, informed members are in direct proportion to the quality of the committee. That is common sense. Many leaders apparently have done a poor job of appointing the right members to committees. I know I have. "Quality begets quality" and "garbage in, garbage out" are two truths we need to keep in the back of our mind.

There is such a thing as a gray decision. That is a decision made by unqualified and inexperienced but well-meaning folks or those who make decisions based on offending as few people as possible. To make good decisions, have the fortitude to do what is correct—not what is popular. Gray decisions are decisions made for the wrong reasons. These gray decisions can be dangerous and detrimental to the company, nonprofit, individual, and so on.

Unfortunately, bad decisions are part of being a change agent and a leader, and they happen more often than desired. Bad decisions are made many times by qualified individuals or committees. Sometimes these qualified groups and individuals look at all the data and still come up with the wrong solutions. We've all made bad decisions at times, but we can learn from them. Learning from mistakes is important. I have learned a lot from many of mine. However, mistakes can be an expensive, time-consuming, and demoralizing way to learn. When you discover your mistake, go through the proper procedures to correct it quickly, and then move on. It sounds easy, but we all know it is not. Eating crow is not fun for anyone.

Sometimes we fear making a decision because we do not have a decision-making plan. Here's a decision-making plan that I use:

Write down your plan. Use an outline style for the steps, or perhaps you would rather use a decision tree or a graph. You could also combine any of the above styles. Use any method you prefer. The important thing is to put it on paper.

1. Make sure you are calm and collected when you make your final decision.
2. Always look to your moral compass. Let's say you're making a business decision. Do the options fit with your personal values and your company's values, vision, and mission? Can you proudly look in the mirror the next day and be excited about your action?
3. Look at all the facts, and listen to what your feelings and emotions are telling you.
4. Try to see your decision as a resolution of the situation. If it is not, find out why. Try hard to avoid the Band-Aid approach.
5. Clearly define the situation. Know all the variables you will consider in making your decision. For example, let's say you are going to buy a house. That defines what the decision is all about.

Some variables to consider when buying a home might be as follows:

a. Location, location, location
b. Square footage
c. Price
d. Must-have amenities (large yard, lots of light, terrace, fireplace, etc.)
e. Style of home
f. Financing
g. Real-estate agent
h. Central heat and air
i. Gas appliances

6. Make a list of the pros and cons of the decision. What if two pros carry the same weight? Flip a coin? No way. Study both, and you will eventually decide that one is a little better than the other. There are always differences between two positive decisions. Your job is to find what they are. This will take effort, and it can be frustrating. Stick with it until you find all of them. Then make the best choice. Make your decision.

7. Make sure you are not just gathering more accurate data in order to procrastinate. You must find the right time to cut off information gathering and start the decision-making process.

8. Always double-check your data for accuracy.

9. Prioritize the list and give more detail under each variable. In the home-buying example, you might list under "Gas appliances" that you want a gas line instead of a tank. Under "Amenities," you might write that the fireplace must be natural wood—not gas logs.

10. Have confidence in your decision-making ability. Look back on all the correct decisions you have made in the past. When the accurate facts and your gut tell you this is what you should do, make the decision.

The following true story is an example of being just the opposite of calm when making a decision. Back in the seventies, I was a young man running a regional marketing-and-advertising agency. Our local sheriff hired me to handle his reelection campaign; I had also handled his first one. We set up a meeting for two o'clock the next afternoon to go over some reelection plans.

I arrived early, but the sheriff called to say he would be running late. While I waited, I talked with the radio dispatcher. I should specify now that the sheriff's office was located in the same building as the county jail at that time.

All of a sudden, the heavy steel door to the jail section slammed open with a loud boom. A prisoner stood there holding a .38 pistol, and it was aimed straight at me and the radio dispatcher. It was an armed jailbreak. We both held our hands up. I just stood there, but the dispatcher slid from the chair he was sitting in down under his desk—a wise move on his part. The armed prisoner ran out the front door as fast as he could and headed down the street. The armed dispatcher jumped up, handed me a twelve-gauge shotgun, ran out the door, and chased after the escapee. He yelled back, "Get some help. Quick!"

All this happened in less than two minutes. To say the least, I was rattled. I was very scared that other prisoners would come through that open steel door to escape as well.

My job, though, was to get help. I went over to the desk, pressed down on a red mic button, and did all I could think to do. I got on that microphone, and in a very loud and shaky voice, I hollered, "Mayday! Mayday!" Then I said it again.

I heard a reply from the chief deputy, Charles Long. "What is going on?" I told him who I was and that there had been a jailbreak. He said, "I am on my way, but it will take me about twenty minutes. Call the local police. Their office is less than a mile away."

I said, "OK, but I don't know how to use this radio to call them."

In a very loud voice, he said, "Use the telephone!"

For months after that, my nickname was "Super Cop." I was so rattled that I had not even thought of the telephone. Try not to make important decisions under great stress, fear, or both. As shown above, there are exceptions to the rule. I hope you will be able to think under great pressure better than I did that day.

Later that day, the escapee was recaptured. The recapture of the prisoner is a story I have already told you about in an earlier chapter of the book. As you might remember, I was involved in the prisoner's recapture. All in all, it was one stressful day.

Decision-making during change or any other time always involves a moral component. You must be determined to do the right thing. This is not always as easy as it seems—no matter how much moral character you possess. There are usually some resisters to any decision you make. Sometimes their resistance can be significant. You must make the best decision based on what is morally correct, and that is often not the most popular choice.

The Tennessee Valley Authority (TVA) is a US government agency that was established back in the 1930s to provide electrical power to the Tennessee Valley. This huge valley includes parts of several states.

When the agency began, the TVA built dams that backed up rivers. This formed lakes for supplying water to power generators in the dams that made electricity in the region, and it helped with flooding in the valley. The TVA had to buy many farms and homes where the lakes would be formed. Some of the property was purchased under the eminent-domain statute.

To offend as few people as possible, the TVA went to extremes to accommodate landowners who were forced to move from their properties. One elderly lady insisted that the fire in her fireplace be moved to her new home. The TVA went to the expense of building a fireplace in her new residence and actually transferred the fire as requested; the new home was about eight miles away from the old residence. This was the only way the woman would agree to move without court action. The reason she gave for insisting on this was that she had had a continuous fire in the existing fireplace for over fifty years. She and her family were very proud of that fact.

Why did the TVA do this? Was it a good use of tax dollars? The answer is a resounding yes. Here's why. If the agency had been forced to go to court, the sympathy for the woman's situation would have been great enough that the TVA would likely have had to pay far more than the actual value of the land. However, the biggest reason was that the case could have stayed in court for several years and delayed the opening of the entire project.

By accommodating this elderly lady and her family, the TVA was able to please everyone involved and supply electricity and flood protection to the whole area on schedule. It was a win-win solution for all involved, and that included the taxpayers and the people of the region.

For the record, the regional press tried to make a laughingstock out of the TVA for wasting money and time. Doing what is best for all is not always understood by the general public, your family, or your employees. Instead of becoming a joke, the TVA's move was a public-relations and money-saving masterstroke. The people in this region of Tennessee sincerely appreciated what the TVA had done for this elderly lady, and the action enhanced the TVA's goodwill in the area.

You must first make a plan and then work the plan. There is a lot of decision-making necessary to accomplish both. Let's look at how important planning is to success. Here are some quotes to help make a solid case for planning:

> *By failing to prepare, you are preparing to fail.*
> —BENJAMIN FRANKLIN

> *Think ahead. Don't let day-to-day*
> *operations drive out planning.*
> —DONALD RUMSFELD

> *A goal without a plan is just a wish.*
> —ANTOINE DE SAINT-EXUPÉRY

> *In preparing for battle I have always found that*
> *plans are useless, but planning is indispensable.*
> —DWIGHT EISENHOWER

> *If you don't know where you are going,*
> *you'll end up someplace else.*
> —YOGI BERRA

> *Never look back unless you are planning to go that way.*
> —HENRY DAVID THOREAU

It takes as much energy to wish as it does to plan.
—ELEANOR ROOSEVELT

Many people spend more time in planning the wedding than they do in planning the marriage.
—ZIG ZIGLAR

It pays to plan ahead. It wasn't raining when Noah built the ark.
—ANONYMOUS

Happy people plan actions, they don't plan results.
—DENNIS WHOLEY

Plans are only good intentions unless they immediately degenerate into hard work.
—PETER F. DRUCKER

Good fortune is what happens when opportunity meets with planning.
—THOMAS ALVA EDISON

Planning is a must. So many of us know how important planning is but never have enough time to do all of it. The solution is to take the time anyway. Never go into any situation (personal or business related) that you do not plan for in advance. If you want to be a consistent winner, you must plan.

Now, let's get back to the subject of great decision-making. In decision-making, the goal is to make the best decision possible, implement the decision with courage, and then move on. Sometimes this is not as easy as it sounds.

Here are some interesting quotes about decision-making. I was surprised how few I was able to find that made sense to me. I hope these inspire you as they have me.

Peacefulness follows any decision, even the wrong one.
—RITA MAE BROWN

*When you have to make a choice and don't
make it, that is, in itself, a choice.*
—WILLIAM JAMES

*Some persons are very decisive when it
comes to avoiding decisions.*
—BRENDAN FRANCIS

*When one bases his life on principle, 99 percent
of his decisions are already made.*
—ANONYMOUS

Life is the sum of all your choices.
—ALBERT CAMUS

*The hardest thing to learn in life is which
bridge to cross and which to burn.*
—DAVID RUSSELL

Indecision becomes decision with time.
—ANONYMOUS

*Do not plant your dreams in the field of indecision,
where nothing ever grows but the weeds of "what if."*
—DODINSKY

*Good decisions come from experience, and
experience comes from bad decisions.*
—ANONYMOUS

*The inability to make a decision has often
been passed off as patience.*
—ANONYMOUS

*Stay committed to your decisions, but
stay flexible in your approach.*
—TOM ROBBINS

Indecision and delays are the parents of failure.
—GEORGE CANNING

*In a moment of decision, the best thing you can do is the
right thing to do. The worst thing you can do is nothing.*
—THEODORE ROOSEVELT

*When a decision has to be made, make it. There
is no totally right time for anything.*
—GENERAL GEORGE PATTON

*We know what happens to people who stay in
the middle of the road. They get run over.*
—ANEURIN BEVAN

Making decisions is something we do every day. Since we make decisions all the time, you would think we would be better at making big decisions. The sooner you learn to go through the decision-making plan or process correctly and make the decision, the sooner you will feel relief. I strongly suggest we all stop thinking up excuses and get the correct processes started. Anytime change occurs, we will have decisions to make.

Why do most of us fear making decisions? Most of the decisions we make during an average day do not affect a lot of people or have serious consequences. Decisions we make regularly are not in the public eye, and they are generally the type we have made many times before. For example, if I choose a lunch item that does not taste good, the consequence is that I have a lunch I don't enjoy. On the other hand, if I pick the wrong university to attend, it could be of momentous consequence. We often procrastinate because of the fear of failure and the embarrassment it can bring.

For almost twenty years, I was president and chairperson of the board at a bank. Sometimes, I would personally look at property we were considering for a loan. On one occasion, I was looking at a farm whose owner was applying for a loan. When I drove up to the farmhouse, I could see an elderly gentleman sitting on his front porch. As I got out of the car, I waved to him and asked, "Sir, have you lived here all your life?"

The older gentleman shouted back to me these exact words: "No, not yet!" Not only was this humorous, but it was revealing. This one short phrase told me a great deal about this man's character. He had told me of his future plans; he was here for the long haul. Although I had a good idea that his character was excellent, I still made sure the proper steps were followed, and his loan was approved. I had been tempted to approve his loan on the spot, but I did not. One of the keys to making solid decisions about change or anything else is discipline. Discipline is a friend, and you must never forget to use it.

Most of the fear in decision-making is the fear of potential failure. The right move is to have a plan for making decisions that you trust and believe in strongly. Success is all about making decisions. Notice that I did not say making great decisions. Successful people often make wrong decisions before they make correct ones. They learn from their bad decisions and try again. They do not give up without working their decision plans again.

Perfection is not possible. Decision-making is choosing the best of the alternatives you have discovered. Making almost any decision is a calculated risk. Have the courage to make the decision. As Davy Crockett said, "Be sure you are right and then go ahead."

After you have made your decision, you can expect to have problems to solve implementing that decision and that is normal. In the next chapter learn about problem- solving the correct way.

CHAPTER 11

Problem-Solving During Change: Understanding Leads to Solving the Problem

There is nothing wrong with change,
if it is in the right direction.
—WINSTON CHURCHILL

Winning by being a great problem solver will take you where you want to go. Formulating a plan to solve a specific problem begins with describing in detail the problem to be solved. The *Harvard Business Review* says, "You can't collaborate unless you agree on the problem." That is just common sense, but over the years, how many groups, teams, and individuals either did not take the time to do that or assumed everyone knew all about the problem? If groups or teams do attempt to talk about the problem to be solved, they seldom go into enough detail.

All successful problem-solving requires a lot of solid thinking. You should never forget to use that wonderful tool you have between your ears—no matter how big or how small the idea might be. How many of us often act before we have thought long and hard about our proposed actions? We must always get all the facts before we attempt to ponder our solutions.

A neighbor of mine once acted before thinking through the process. One afternoon, she called the mayor's office to request the removal of the deer-crossing sign on our street. She gave this reason: "Too many deer are being hit by cars out here. I don't think this is a good place for them to cross anymore." My neighbor is not dumb. She just did not think before she took action. Think, think, and then think again. Then—and only then—should you take action.

In defining the problem, make sure you address the actual problem. If your workforce is not cutting pieces of wood correctly, it might not be the employees' fault. The saw blade could be misaligned, or perhaps the table and the saw do not line up. Find the real problem that needs to be fixed before you start. Do not waste time and money fixing a symptom of the real problem. The problem is not the worker; it's the table and the saw. Fail to identify the real problem, and at best, you can expect many wrong suggestions. At worst, you will end up spending time, money, and effort trying to solve the wrong problem or a problem that does not exist. As a consultant, I have seen this happen rather often. Leave nothing to chance. Always start with a detailed explanation of the real problem, and let the team ask questions about it. Know the real problem like you know the back of your hand. If you do that, you are well on your way to success.

Here is a five-step process for problem-solving:

1. Identify the real problem.
2. Write out a plan for fixing the real problem.
3. Write out a plan for implementing the fix once the real problem is discovered.
4. Fix the real problem by following the written implementation plan.
5. Test the fixed problem to make sure it has been totally corrected. Check back from time to time. Even better, have specific dates and times to check back to see if the fix is still working correctly.

When your plan is fully implemented, take another look at your overall system. See if you find other situations with the same problem. Make very sure it is the exact same problem. This means you can use the same fix plan. Taking the original change plan and adapting it to the same problem in other parts of the company is a great time-and-money saver. Repeat as often as needed until all the same problems have been fixed throughout the company. It is a win-win situation—for you, the employees involved, and the company.

Management should initiate and encourage these celebrations. Have a big party with all of management present—and, yes, have a great time. You and the team deserve it. This is the time to pat yourself on the back. Pat the backs of others involved too. Give special attention to those who have delivered especially outstanding performances. Have a fun party— not a meeting with a lot of speeches and formality. That is a definite no-no. Celebrating is an important part of the overall process, and the party should be festive and fun for the team members. This party is for and about the team members. Make sure that what you do at the party is something that will please the team members. At one party I attended, the grand-prize drawing was for two rounds of golf at the company president's private country club. Was it a great grand prize? No. The team members were 80 percent blue-collar workers, and 75 percent of them did not play golf. Management thought it would be a great grand prize because it appealed to them. Most of management would have loved to be offered the grand prize. In this case, the grand prize was a big flop.

Solving problems requires excellent communication skills. What are some solid proven ways to communicate? Let us find out in the next chapter.

CHAPTER 12

Communication and Change-Management

> *You cannot control what happens to you,*
> *but you can control your attitude*
> *toward what happens to you, and in that, you will be mastering*
> *change rather than allowing it to master you.*
> —BRIAN TRACY

By now, it should be clear that change management is a people business. Unless all management understands change—that is, fully understands the change being planned—in all probability, that change will not succeed. At the beginning, it might seem that the resisters have the upper hand. To counteract that, you must be an excellent communicator. All change agents must be quality leaders, and all good leaders know how to communicate well to one or a group of people. Here are some common mistakes that communicators and change agents make in the communication process:

1. They are not good listeners.
2. They are not fully prepared.
3. They do not communicate face-to-face with groups or individuals. Instead, they deliver good (and especially bad) news by e-mail or post to a bulletin board.
4. They beat around the bush when problems arise and do not face issues head-on or in the open.

5. They do not participate in plan-related celebrations and by that communicate that they are not team players in some eyes.
6. They are not enthusiastic about the project, or they give that appearance.
7. They use a cookie-cutter approach. They believe everyone will act the same way to the same stimuli.
8. They have a "my way or the highway" approach and do not listen to or take suggestions from the group or individuals.
9. They do not ask questions to find out where the group is on the learning and buying-in process.

There are many other common errors in communication. This list should give you a general idea of the things not to do.

One of the main pillars of the change process is good communication practices. A change agent or anyone in a leadership role should have good communication skills in abundance. What other attributes should good change agents and leaders possess? In addition to being good communicators, they should be likeable. They should be able to make friends easily and enjoy being with people from all segments of the company's staff—from management to the hourly worker. You will not find these qualities listed on a person's résumé. No matter how knowledgeable someone is, if he or she cannot pass the likability test, that person should not be the leader of the change process. Here are six more must-haves of solid communicators to round out the package:

1. They are always clear and concise. To good communicators, this is second nature. Here are two true examples from paraphrased conversations between Lady Astor and Winston Churchill. As you may remember, they had a great dislike for each other. They both demonstrate being clear and concise.
   a. At a cocktail party: "Winston, you are drunk."
   b. "Yes, I am drunk, and you are ugly. Tomorrow I will be sober, and you will still be ugly."
   c. Later at the same party: "Winston, if you were my husband, I would put poison in your coffee."
   d. "And, madam, if I were your husband, I would drink it."

2. Good communicators are great listeners.
3. Excellent communicators need a teacher persona and the patience of Job.
4. Communicators you want to listen to have a great attitude.
5. They genuinely enjoy being with and among people.
6. They have a lot of enthusiasm and are full of energy.

I remember when ice cream cost about fifteen cents a scoop at Walgreens. Back then, I used to hear a story about a nine-year-old boy sitting down at a table as a server put a glass of water in front of him. "How much is an ice-cream sundae?" he asked.

"Fifty cents," replied the server.

The little boy pulled his hand out of his pocket and studied the coins in it. "Well, how much is a plain scoop of ice cream?"

By now, more people were waiting for tables, and the server was growing impatient. "Thirty-five cents," she brusquely replied.

The little boy again counted his coins. "I'll have the scoop," he said.

The server brought the ice cream, put the bill on the table, and abruptly walked away. The boy finished the ice cream, paid the cashier, and left. When the server came back to that table, she began to cry as she wiped down the table. There, placed neatly beside the empty dish, were two nickels and five pennies. You see, he couldn't have the sundae because he had to have enough left to leave her a tip.

Sometimes the action a person takes might not seem correct, but it is right on target. Make sure you get all the facts before making a judgment. The waitress made a decision about the young boy that was in error. She wished she had been more patient. Patience is a virtue that I could use more of on a regular basis. In order to be an excellent leader, you need to have a lot of patience. I have learned much from others by using my limited patience to hear them out. Patience is a huge positive in good communication.

All of us communicate every day. This does not mean all of us are good at this important skill. A good communicator does not put up barriers; he or she does the opposite. The good communicator fights barriers that others raise. Expect to do that often in implementing the change process. The communicator is keenly aware that everyone assimilates data at a different pace and knows that feedback should be solicited. If any part of the plan is not clear to the hearer, the communicator will take all the time necessary to make the situation crystal clear to that person or group. The best way to discern that is to ask questions of the audience or individual. The following old story is a good example of how your audience can get confused about something you thought was clear.

A minister decided that a visual demonstration would add emphasis to his Sunday sermon. He placed four earthworms into four separate jars. The first worm was put into a container of alcohol. The second worm was put into a container of cigarette smoke. The third worm was put into a container of chocolate syrup. The fourth worm was put into a container of good, clean soil. At the conclusion of the long sermon, he reported the following results: The first worm, in alcohol, was dead. The second worm, in cigarette smoke, was dead. The third worm, in chocolate syrup, was dead. The fourth worm, in the clean soil, was alive and doing well. The minister asked the congregation, "What did you learn from the demonstration?" There was a moment of silence. Then Maxine, who was sitting in the back, raised her hand and said, "As long as you drink, smoke, and eat chocolate, you won't have worms?" That pretty much ended the Sunday service. It is clear the minister had some work to do. Make sure your audience gets it. The speaker never leaves the audience confused. That can cause fear and anxiety and make things worse. The good communicator takes the time to get it right.

The expert communicator knows he or she must be an excellent listener. It's the only way to know what people do and do not understand. After you listen, you can go back and explain the problematic portion of a written or verbal communication again. Few things turn a person off more than someone who does not listen to them or does not take what they say seriously. Become a great listener, and you are well on your way to becoming a great communicator.

Here are some other ways to be a good communicator and a great listener:

1. Use positive body language. This is a key to letting the individual or group know you are listening and are interested in what is being said. In listening, body language is 100 percent of communication. Positive body language is as follows:

a. Maintain an open posture. Do not cross your arms. Keep your arms by your sides in an open and friendly position.
b. Nod your head from time to time to let the person doing the talking know you are listening.
c. Face the person who is speaking.
d. Make eye contact with the person who is speaking, if possible.
e. Use facial expressions to let the person know you are listening. Smile, raise your eyebrows, and so on.
f. Use small verbal statements to show you are listening. For example, say, "Yes," "I see," or "Uh-huh."

2. Keep an open mind. That way, you can hear all that is being said. Shut out all other distractions if possible.

3. Do not think about anything but the current conversation. Do not plan your next remark while you are listening.

4. Always treat the speaker with respect and courtesy, no matter how much you might agree or disagree with what that person is saying.

5. Do not lose your cool, regardless of what the other party says. Showing anger is a mistake. It will make you look small and can cause a breakdown in communication. Here is an example of how to not show anger but at the same time make your point. This is a true story. When Senator Edmund Muskie was campaigning for the vice presidency way back in 1968, he often told the story of a big Texas rancher bragging about how big his ranch was to a farmer from Maine. "My ranch is so big that it takes me five whole days just to drive around the outside of it," said the Texas rancher. The Maine farmer quickly retorted, "Know what you mean. I had a car like that once."

6. Do not interrupt. No one wins when you interrupt the speaker. Let him or her completely finish speaking before you respond.

7. When you speak in rebuttal, let the listener know where you are coming from. For example, preface your statement with, "This is my personal opinion…" or "Here are the facts about…"

8. When someone asks a question of you, it is a good idea to repeat the question to the speaker before you answer it. This is especially true if you are using a mic.

9. When you are unclear about what a person has just said, ask him or her to tell you more. You can clarify what you just heard by asking, "So, are you saying..." or "I heard you say..."

10. Get clarification when you have any doubt. It is important for the listener to understand clearly what has just been said before answering the speaker's remarks. If you do not understand, you may not make any sense.

11. Practice active listening. It takes discipline to be a good listener; it does not come naturally. For most of us, active listening is not something we do well, but practice makes perfect.

12. At least 55 percent of what the other person says is in his or her body language. While actively listening with your ears, you should also be observing the speaker's body language.

13. Listen to more than just words. Listen to how the speaker says something. Voice tone speaks volumes. Remember, this works both ways—when you are listening and when you are speaking.

14. If you are the speaker, let the listener have the spotlight from time to time. You do not have to be the speaker all the time to get your message across to others. When you let others have attention, they will be more forthcoming and more passionate about being on your team and on your side.

15. Always listen fully. Listening is a full-time job. There is no reason to think about anything but listening while listening. Never try to listen to someone while doing something else. Giving your full attention to the speaker is the only way to hear all that is being said. Not doing so is rude.

16. Keep your mind completely open to what the other person is saying. This is not always easy. How can you communicate correctly if you do not know where the other person is coming from? You need to understand a person's point of view fully before you can intelligently agree or disagree with that person.

If you have made a serious mistake in listening or in any other realm and must make amends, here are some tips for recovering from your error:

1. Take full responsibility for your actions. Be frank about what happened, and tell the whole story. Do not hold back. You might say something like, "This is entirely my fault." You could also try, "I made the error."
2. Apologize as quickly as you can. Stop the bleeding, the complaining, and the defensive moves of other group members. Nip discontent in the bud as quickly as possible.
3. If team members complain, listen carefully. Do not interrupt. Let them get the problem off their chests. Pause before you respond.
4. Make sure you understand the complaint completely. If you do not, ask leading questions—for example, "Can you tell me more about that?" or "Let me see if I have your statement right."
5. Never respond defensively.
6. Offer a well-prepared and researched solution. Take the time to do this slowly. Do not rush the explanation or the solution.
7. Welcome questions at any time during the process, but especially welcome them during your explanation of how the problem occurred and your response in correcting the problem. Make sure you do not sound like a martyr or as if you want a pity party. Do not let either feeling sneak into your communication.
8. Know when to have a discussion and when to walk away. If at all possible, pick the right time and place for explaining and discussing the problem you have caused.

When going through these steps for correcting an error you have made, be sure your audience can feel how sincerely sorry you are about it. Your attitude of humility should be shining through as you go through the apology process. I believe quality listening is a virtue. It takes practice and discipline. Not listening causes a lot of confusion. For example, a wife was telling her husband about how much she was looking forward to a milk bath she had planned for the next day at her spa. "Pasteurized?" the husband asked. She said, "No, honey. It only comes up to my navel." This silly story illustrates how easy it is to not hear what is actually being said or asked. The first and last rule in listening is to pay attention to the person who is speaking. Paying attention is often harder than you think—especially if the other person is not a good communicator. How can you answer a question clearly if you do not pay attention to the question? Good listening is a great attribute to have. Take the time to practice it. You will be glad many times over that you did.

This chart shows the tools you use the most when you communicate:

HOW WE COMMUNICATE

Body Language	**55%**
Voice Tone/Inflection	**38%**
Words	**7%**
Total	**100%**

THE SECRET WEAPON IS...

SILENCE

You are communicating even when you're not talking. Listening is the other side of great communication. These tools should be used while listening as well. That is why points on listening are discussed throughout this chapter. All great communicators are good listeners.

Your audience must fully understand the words you are using. The meanings of words can be different based on tone and inflection, body language, or both. Some might find that hard to believe, but this is a rule of communication. Think about it. How many different ways can you mean the word "yes"? I can say "yes" and communicate six different feelings. I am sure you can beat that number. If it is true that voice tone, inflection, and body language make up 93 percent of all communication, then it makes sense that communication can be accomplished without saying a word. My mother used the raised eyebrow to great effect on my sister and me. Trust me; we knew what she meant. Use all three of these communication tools when you have something to say. Great communicators listen 81 percent of the time and speak 19 percent of the time. Listening is a huge part of communicating.

An additional tool that is harder to categorize but that can be very effective when used wisely is silence. You can use a well-timed pause in any conversation or speech and when someone asks a question you think is silly or out of line. Properly executed silence is an excellent communication tool that is often not even considered.

Without well-honed communication skills—and listening is a major one—it is impossible to be an effective leader. To say someone is a good leader but has poor communication skills is an oxymoron.

One requirement of motivating others is solid communications skills. Next how to motivate others is on the agenda.

CHAPTER 13

How to Motivate and Sell People on Change

We must all obey the great law of change.
It is the most powerful law of nature.
—EDMUND BURKE

t might seem odd that leaders need to sell people on embracing positive change. People like positive things happening in their lives. Or do they? This is not necessarily true when the positive event is change. For one thing, they might not see it as a positive.

Change agents are leaders who advocate positive change. To be an effective change agent, you must be able to motivate and sell others on the vision of the planned change. If you do not have a grasp on selling or encouraging positive action, you are likely to fail at your job. Selling and motivating are similar in many respects—but not all. We will look at each of these important skills separately.

First, let me say that all change makes a difference. However, the same change can mean different things to the various individuals in the group. The significance or value of the change might also be different for each person involved. These are important truths to keep in mind when motivating and selling change to your family, staff, or any group or team. Pointing out that you and the group or team are going to make a positive difference when the planned change is implemented is a good selling point.

For example, I have a friend who jogs as part of her overall exercise program. Every Sunday morning, she takes a light jog around a small lake near her home. She shared the following story with me:

Every Sunday, I see the same elderly man sitting at the water's edge with a small metal cage beside him.

This past Sunday, my curiosity got the best of me. I stopped jogging and walked over to this man whom I had seen every week. As I got closer, I realized the metal cage was in fact a small trap. There were three unharmed turtles slowly walking around in it. He had a fourth turtle on his lap that he was carefully scrubbing with a brush.

"Hello," I said. "I see you here every Sunday morning. I'd love to know what you're doing with these turtles."

A big smile came across his face. "I'm cleaning off their shells," he replied. "Anything on a turtle's shell, like algae or scum, reduces the turtle's ability to absorb heat and hinders its ability to swim. It can also weaken the shell over time."

"Good for you," I replied.

He went on, "I spend two or three hours here at the lake each Sunday morning, relaxing and helping these little fellows out. It's my way of making a difference."

"Don't most turtles live their whole lives with scum and algae on their shells?" I asked.

"Yep. Sadly they do."

"Then don't you think your time could be better spent? I think your efforts are noble, but there are turtles living in lakes all around the world. And ninety-nine point nine percent of them don't have nice people like you to help them clean off their shells. No offense…but how exactly are your efforts truly making a difference?"

The man laughed. He looked me in the eye and then down at the turtle in his lap. He scrubbed off the last piece of algae and dirt from its shell and said, "Madam, if this little guy could talk, he'd tell you I just made all the difference in his world to him."

We can change the world—maybe not all at once, but we can do it one person, one animal, and one good deed at a time. Wake up every morning, and be determined to make a difference that day. The more we know about change and how it makes us feel, the easier consistent change is to understand and go through. Making a difference is made easier with a well-grounded knowledge of change. The same change can mean different things to the various members of the group or team. Now, let's talk in detail about selling and motivation.

Selling Others on Positive Change

Most people have ideas about what selling is all about and how to do it. The secret is to be very good at selling without being overbearing. If you do not like selling, my advice is to get over it. This is the most important tool in your communication arsenal. Here are the steps to proper selling in the order they should be accomplished:

1. Be prepared. You must know to whom you are selling the suggested change. Know everything you can about this group or individual. What is that person's state of mind? What needs is that person looking to fulfill? Know the average education level of the group or person. Change always brings some form of anxiety or fear. Know the positives and negatives that will be in store for your audience.

2. Sell yourself first. Take all the time and effort necessary to get this right before you go to the next step. When you do this correctly, you will be well on your way to a positive selling conclusion. People like to buy from others or buy into things from people they like and trust. Sometimes the person doing the selling overlooks trust. You need to prove to the group by your actions that you are a person of high integrity and that you can be trusted. You must have a pleasant attitude and demeanor when you sell change or anything else. If you don't, you start with two (or even three) strikes against you. I know people from whom I would not buy anything they brought to the table—simply because of their bad attitudes in the past or present. Always be conscious of your attitude at work or at play. Here are some basic facts about attitude and selling:
   a. You must have a good attitude.
   b. Body language is important when you first get acquainted with a person or group; it is 55 percent of communication. Make sure you present an open and pleasant stance.
   c. Smiling makes a difference. Do it often.

d. Voice tone is 38 percent of all communication. Make sure yours is pleasant to hear. Make sure it's not too loud or too soft. Speak in conversational tones. Do not use an "announcer voice" but a tone that is crisp and friendly. Some have a tendency to do this when they use a mic.

e. Sell yourself and the message by using words your audience can understand. If you use technical jargon or other unfamiliar words, you might as well be speaking in a foreign language. It is true that words are only 7 percent of communication; however, they fill in the gaps that voice tone and body language cannot communicate. In essence, words describe in specifics what you want to communicate. Of course, words are important to any conversation. Choose them wisely, and the audience will get your message. Get your words wrong, and you'll have a bored and confused group or individual on your hands. I cannot overemphasize the importance of selling yourself.

3. Teach and repeat. You must become a teacher. It is better to overdo it than to leave some in the group lost or confused. All the people in a group will never get it at the same time. Keep asking questions until you have a feel for how many are on board with you at that point. It is normal that some in the group take longer to buy the change plan. If necessary, repeat the positives until you are sick and tired of doing it. It's a pretty good gauge for knowing when the majority understands and can go along with the planned change.

4. Listen to what other people are saying. You do that by listening to the words and the tone of other people's voices and by observing their body language. Listening is a big part of selling. In selling, you might be pleasantly surprised at what your prospect will tell you if you ask the right questions and listen well.

5. According to the 20-50-30 Rule, about 30 percent of the group will resist the plan (now or in the future). Even after you've explained and discussed the plan until you are sick and tired of doing it, a few just will not go along with it. What do we do with these folks? We ignore them.

6. Sell the vision and mission statements after you have sold yourself at the beginning. After all, your team or audience members should have had a hand in designing those statements, so they should be willing to accept them. Again, you will have resisters. Ignore them. Move on to the other 70 percent.

7. Sell the dream. Tell the group often about how things will be better after the planned positive change has been fully implemented and is up and running. Be specific. Talk about feelings, security, and all the positives the change will bring to them as individuals and to the company. Give them solid reasons to go along with the plan. Always speak to a group as if you are speaking to one individual.

8. Never be aggressive. You should be excited and interested in the results the positive change will bring, but do not be pushy. "My way or the highway" does not work in the long run. Negativity does motivate, but that's only in the very short term. It is OK to be assertive. But a hard sell will be unsuccessful generally speaking, and will hurt the plan's chances of being accepted by the majority.

9. Ask questions and welcome questions. The questions you ask as a change agent and leader provide a great way to find out where the group is on any particular subject—what concerns they have with the change plan and its implementation. You will also find that answering questions in full is a good teaching tool. Do not dread questions. See them for what they are—good teaching tools and solid ways to judge where the group is on the learning curve.

10. Celebrate the little things in front of the group as often as you find these positives. Praise will help the attitude of the group and make you more likeable.

11. Reassure. Be a cheerleader. This is an important part of the change agent's job. Keep things positive. There is always something positive going on with the group—no matter how down things might look at the moment. Talk about the positives. Always make sure 100 percent of the management staff backs you. Management should be the cheerleaders from the sidelines.

12. Resisters are complainers. However, not all complaints come from resisters. Do what is necessary to address complaints of those who have problems. The secret is to know who is doing the complaining and ignore the true resisters. When addressing a valid complaint, keep in mind that others in the group might feel the same way as the one doing the complaining. It is a good idea to ask the group after addressing the complaint if the group understands your explanation.

13. Selling a change-management plan should be a learning experience for all those in the group. As the change agent, it is your job to bring along with you as many people as possible. You do that by selling them on the idea behind the change plan. Explain to the group what can happen if no change is implemented, and show them what will happen if the change plan is fully implemented.

Everyone is in some form of sales almost daily. Those who fail to see this truth will not go far in life.

Motivating Others to Embrace Positive Change

At the beginning of this chapter, I pointed out that selling and motivating are similar in some ways, but they are not the same. Selling could be thought of as a form of motivation. *Wiktionary* defines motivation as "providing a reason to act in a certain way." Here is an example of motivation at work:

An army recruiter when talking to someone interested in joining may say statements like:

"Join us because you love your country or because of all the excellent benefits we offer."

A school teacher might say things like:

"This test will count as twenty percent of your grade in this class or you need to read this book because it will help you when you get to college."

Motivation is bringing someone or some group around to your way of thinking. It is convincing someone or some group to act, believe, or understand your mode of thinking and convincing that person to take positive action toward that vision or goal. Synonyms include inspiration, inducement, cause, and impetus. Here are steps to help you motivate an individual or a group. You will notice that many of these steps are similar to the list about sales.

1. Talk about success often and as if it is the only course you know or will consider. Share the big picture.
2. Have a teacher's attitude. See yourself as a teacher who is willing to listen and fill in the gaps in thinking. Do not just dictate the next move or step. Tell stories. Ask questions, and listen to feedback from individuals and the group.
3. Create positive feelings about the project. Knowing the facts puts people at ease. However, a great deal of their motivation will feed off your emotions and enthusiasm. Be upbeat, be positive, and be a good, patient listener.
4. Praise people in public, and do it often. Look for ways to say positive things. We all like praise, so lavish it on the individual or group whenever it's deserved.
5. Smile a lot. This goes along with a positive and friendly attitude. You will be pleased with the smiles you get back when you smile first.
6. When you praise others, be as specific as possible. "Sam, thank you for taking that work home over the weekend" is better than "Good job, Sam."
7. Talk often about the goals, mission, and vision of the project. In all my company meetings, the first thing on the agenda is the reading of the company's vision and mission statements. At our meetings now, staff members will often repeat the statements aloud when they are read, even though they are not required to do so.
8. Give from your heart. Motivation is a heart game more than it is a mind game; it is mostly about appealing to the emotions of your audience.

9. Give feedback often. Let people know how they are doing. Let them know where they are right now in the change-management process. Groups and individuals who do not know where they are in the process will naturally feel lost. This can cause dissension in the ranks and can lower morale.

10. Celebrate milestones and successes. Literally have a party. Let people know they are appreciated. This has been mentioned several times in this book because it is so important.

11. Treat people as the individuals they are. Not everyone needs the same kind or amount of motivation. Make sure team members do not fall between the cracks. Mix it up.

12. Let the folks know they have ownership in the project and that the work they have done and will be doing on this change project is important and meaningful.

The exciting thing about motivation is that everyone enjoys being treated that way. The important thing is to make very sure that the motivation you provide is positive and enjoyable. Be sensitive to the group's feelings about the positive emotions you are presenting. If you sense that the plan you have started is not working, change it quickly or start over. For me, few things are more exciting and exhilarating than leading and being led by positive motivation.

Next you will learn about negotiating skills. You can never be a solid negotiator unless you know how to motivate and sell to others. This important skill is one you will need in your journey to more success.

CHAPTER 14

The Art of Negotiation

I understand the importance of the negotiation.
It is a collective act.
—THOM MAYNE

We all negotiate all the time. Deciding which movie to see or what restaurant to choose for dinner can be forms of negotiation. If you have children in your home, you probably negotiate with them several times a day. We should be familiar with negotiating. In fact, it seems as if it should be second nature. It is not. Most of us do not know the ins and outs of how to negotiate correctly. You and I will generally fear or dislike those things we do not understand. Especially for important negotiations, be sure you have the knowledge and experience to accomplish the job and win—or get an expert to do it for you. Inexperience in a negotiation can be embarrassing and potentially cause a disaster for you, your business, or others.

Shortly after I graduated from the University of Tennessee, I became president of a bank in our community. I had a real-estate broker's license, and I had an attorney friend who asked me to testify in a case against the state of Tennessee. I was to serve as an appraiser for his client. His client was involved in a lawsuit against Tennessee over a piece of property. The attorney representing Tennessee and I knew each other as well. As I was on the witness stand, the attorney for the state of Tennessee asked some preliminary questions, such as where I had gone to college. He asked me when I had graduated. He echoed my answers:

"You graduated about nine months ago." I said yes. He complimented me on my graduation and asked if I had a Tennessee real-estate license and for how long. I told him I did and that the license had been awarded to me about six months ago.

"Mr. Masengill," he said, "let me make sure I have my facts right. You graduated from the University of Tennessee nine months ago, and you passed your broker's exam about six months ago." He looked at the judge and jury and said in a loud voice, "Mr. Masengill, based on your vast experience, what is the amount of your appraisal?"

I could hear a slight chuckle in the courtroom. We won the case, but it was not because of me or my vast experience. You must have knowledge of negotiation and solid experience in this art before you ever attempt an important negotiation. Until you have that, let an expert with the knowledge and experience do it for you.

Many refer to negotiation as an art. Negotiation is a deliberative act or process whose purpose is to find agreement. Here is an example of a good negotiation:

A Philadelphia businessman had to go to New York to take care of some company business, and his wife asked if she could come along.

"But I'll be tied up in conference all the time, dear. You wouldn't enjoy it at all."

"Oh, that's all right; I can spend all my time shopping for clothes while we are there."

"That's silly. You can get anything you want right here."

The wife said with a big smile, "Oh, wonderful. That's what I hoped you would say."

This lady is smooth and knows how to negotiate.

In his inaugural address, President John F. Kennedy said, "Let us never fear to negotiate." He then said, "Let us never negotiate out of fear." I consider that great advice from the former president. In a negotiation, you must be willing to walk away. You always need that tool available to you. If you cannot walk away, you have at least two strikes against you or perhaps even three before you begin.

How can we negotiate and win? Here are thirty important tips for negotiating to win:

1. Know the other side. Two-thirds of the people you will meet are poor negotiators. That is a lot of people. Fifty percent of people dislike the art of negotiating and are uncomfortable and unsettled when they have to negotiate. You need to know all you can about the people you will be negotiating with. Know their likes, dislikes, temperaments, and personality types. Are they good or bad negotiators? Are they experienced at dealing with people? Are they assertive or passive? Are they results driven or more laid-back? Are they micromanagers or delegators? You might think of other attributes to discover. General Patton said something to the effect of, "Until I know my enemy like the back of my hand, I am not ready to fight the fight."

2. Be prepared. Like a good student, always do your homework. Collect the data you need on the person who will be on the other side. Collect all the other data you will need. That includes your company's bottom line before walking. Know what you want from the negotiation. Do this well, and you will have more confidence and will impress the other side. Most important, you will be ready to address any issue the other side brings up. Take this seriously, and give it all the time and study necessary. Here's a true story about being prepared:

    While I was a student at the University of Tennessee, I signed up for a marketing class taught by Professor Carl Cottum. Dr. Cottum gave what he called "oral pop quizzes." In every class, he would call on someone randomly to answer a question about that day's assigned lesson. If the student answered correctly, he or she received an A on the oral quiz. If the student answered almost correctly, Dr. Cottum might give the student anything from a B to an F.

    One cold Monday morning after a Tennessee-versus-Alabama football game that weekend—which UT won—I went to class. Of course, the entire campus, me included, had celebrated long and hard all weekend. It had been the biggest game of the season for both teams. So there I sat in Dr. Cottum's 8:00 a.m. class. I had not studied the assigned lesson, and I knew nothing about the topic for that day. You guessed it. Dr. Cottum called on me for the oral pop quiz. I had no idea what the answer was and didn't know what to do. Then I thought, marketing is a general kind of subject. If I don't try to answer at all, I will get an F. If I try to answer—even though I know nothing—I might get a C or a D. So I rambled on for a good two or three minutes for my so-called answer, and I was rather proud of my efforts.

When I finished, Dr. Cottum stood up from his desk and paused for what felt like an eternity. He finally looked straight at me. Then he looked at the person sitting in the seat directly in front of me and asked him, "Mr. Crossman, did any of that get on you?" The class burst into laughter. I never tried that again in Dr. Cottum's class. Of course, I got an F on that oral pop quiz.

The moral of the story is this: if you are not prepared, do not ever get up in front of a group and act as if you are prepared!

Each negotiation will be different. There are no cookie-cutter methods to win, other than gathering all the pertinent data and studying that data until you know it well. Collect factual data and more factual data. Give the other side all the data you have that helps make your point. Inundate the other side with it. Quantity will override quality. When your opponent looks over your mountain of favorable data, he or she will be reading about your point of view. This will indirectly influence the opponent. Be very familiar with all the data, because you might get questions about it during the negotiation.

3. Know exactly what you want, what you will and will not negotiate, and why. You need to know the same for the other side. What does the other side want from your side? How do you learn that? Check out the person or company's past history when negotiating.

4. Meet on neutral ground. This is an important step that many leave out. If you meet on your turf, the other side will feel like a fish out of water. It works the other way too. The meeting place should be somewhere that all parties feel comfortable. It must be quiet and have no one coming in or going out of the room. Many times, when the person on the other side is, for example, an

attorney, he or she will want to meet at his or her office, because there is an available room just for this purpose. Do not take that offer. Make sure you meet on neutral ground—even if you must rent a location. I have made this mistake, and let me assure you that you do not want to meet on someone else's home turf.

5. Have a positive attitude. Be friendly, and sell yourself first. Come across as likeable but firm and willing to listen. Then actually listen. Do not work on putting your thoughts together while the other person talks.

6. Ask for more than you will be happy with. This does not mean you should go just a little higher than the lowest price you will accept. Give yourself some wiggle room. Go for a price higher than the one you would be delighted with.

7. Pinpoint what you want. Be simple and direct. Be sure to speak about everything you want and when you want it. Leave nothing out. These are demands, but do not let them sound harsh when you make them. Make them in a conversational tone.

8. Establish trust. There must be trust on both sides, or all could be lost before you start.

9. Ask for what you want. The best way to get what you want is to ask for it. You might be surprised at the answer. You might even get more than you asked for. Asking for something also requires your opponent to make a decision, and that can save time.

10. Set very clear time-and-date deadlines in your demands. Don't accept unreasonable deadlines from the other side. If necessary, negotiate an acceptable date-and-time deadline before you move on to the next point.

11. Listen. Listening is 80 percent of all good communication. It is interesting sometimes what the other side will reveal if you listen closely. Use your body language to demonstrate to the other side that you care about what he or she is saying. It shows you are trying to understand his or her point of view, and this helps create credibility.

12. Ask open-ended questions. Open-ended questions are those that cannot be answered with a simple yes or no. Plan your questions in advance, and ask many of them. Those questions are a

great way to find out where your adversary is coming from. It also shows that you want his or her input and respect his or her needs. It helps keep the dialogue going.

13. Speak in a language the other side will understand. Speak with confidence and in a conversational tone. Deal with the facts, and bring out the facts that support your side. Sometimes I must ask my attorneys and CPAs to speak in a language I can understand. These professionals should know better.

14. Respond; do not react. It is important that the other side never see you sweat. Do not get angry. Instead, build rapport and trust. This is not always easy, but make sure you do it every time. Lose your temper once, and you have lost the upper hand. When possible, create a friendly, problem-solving climate. The correct attitude can make all the difference.

15. See the negotiation as a learning experience. When you settle disagreements in a negotiation, you can also educate yourself about another view of the problem that might have some merit. Although this is not the purpose or goal of the negotiation, it is a side benefit of doing the job correctly.

16. Use concessions as a tool. If you must make a concession, always make sure you get something you want in return. For example, you might say, "Yes, I can do that if you make the payment plan forty-eight months long."

17. Use likability and fear together. Likability and fear are excellent tools to get what you want. Try to be likeable all the time—even in times of disagreement. Use fear sparingly. For example, give the other side hints you might be ready to walk, or let the other side know with body language that you are bored. Remember, a negative stimulus is more effective than a positive one, but that's only in the extreme short run. When you use fear as a motivator, your likability factor goes down in the short run. No one likes bad news, and often the messenger gets some of the blame.

18. Use the "red herring" tool. Put something in your list of demands that you can easily live without. When you are asked to give something up, choose that. You'll look reasonable, and that will create goodwill.

19. Acknowledge that emotions and feelings count by showing both. Show the other side that you are caring and compassionate. Let your opponents know that you care deeply about what you are negotiating. Let them know you fully understand their points of view. If you don't, you could be negotiating about the wrong thing.

20. Use urgency as a tool. State indirectly that time is running out, and if it does, the other side will end up with nothing. The other side is then more likely to give you what you want. Keep the pressure up, but do it carefully. The other side should not feel you are taking the old "my way or the highway" approach. The psychology of this tool is that you must get all you can, because the opportunity is ending. A sign that says "Sale Ends Today" makes people more motivated to buy.

21. Set upper and lower limits for yourself. You must know the high side of what you want. What would make you very happy with the negotiated deal? You must also know the lowest you would accept. Never go below that point. If you don't get it, you should walk. The other side should not know your limits. If the other side finds out, you have lost the negotiation.

22. Avoid setting false expectations. Never let the opposition believe you will not go below your opening offer. Hold firm. However, this is a negotiation—not an ultimatum. If the other side believes this is your final number, the opposition might walk. Then everybody loses.

23. Realize that patience is a virtue. At certain times, you must move slowly in the negotiation process. Listen to what the other side is saying. I have found over the years that there is a definite place and time to be assertive. However, being patient often reaps a bigger reward.

24. Do not give the impression that you are ready for settlement unless you are ready for settlement. When settlement is reached, do not assume you have changed any minds of the opposition.

25. Understand how the end of the negotiation will affect all parties. The end of negotiation means change. In fact, change happens throughout a negotiation. Feelings of loss, anxiety, anger, or fear

might be going on in the minds of all parties. Understanding how change makes people feel is a solid advantage.

26. Make it a team effort. It is important to let the other side see you as someone who is working with a team to accomplish a goal. Maintain an atmosphere that suggests you are there to come to an agreeable solution. The negotiations will run more smoothly, and you will reach a mutually satisfactory conclusion quicker.

27. Speak only with decision-makers. If the group or person on the other side has no decision-making authority, don't negotiate; walk away.

28. Reiterate the agreement. When you have reached an agreement, make it crystal clear what you have agreed to do. Put it in writing along with how and when (deadlines) it will be carried out. Do not let the other side put this task off until a later date. Without a total understanding of what the parties have agreed to, you have accomplished nothing. In fact, you've accomplished less than nothing. No matter how tired and worn out you might be, do not get up from the table until this gets done, everyone completely understands, and all parties have signed and dated the agreement document. Distribute copies of the agreement to all parties at that time. As Casey Stengel said, "It ain't over until it's over." When you have done these things, it is over, but only then.

29. Take a calculated risk. All negotiations are calculated risks. When you go into a room, no one knows what the outcome will be. However, unlike many competitions, this one can have a win-win ending. That's not always possible; there is usually a winner and a loser. However, as long as both groups see themselves as winners, all is well. When this doesn't happen, one side or the other might cry foul. The chances of that are lower, though, if both sides trust each other and if the outcome is in writing and signed by all parties.

30. Speak first. According to a study by the Harvard Business School, you should always attempt to go first. The first five minutes of a negotiation are the most important, according to the *Journal of Applied Sciences*. You should make your points, especially about price, first. This is a controversial recommendation, however.

Some communication experts say just the opposite. If the other person also insists on going first, you should insist on flipping a coin to see who gets that advantage. I believe there are advantages to going first, and here is why:

a. It shows confidence and power to the other side.
b. You get to set the tone for the negotiation. This is important.
c. You start out in control.
d. You get to "anchor" the parameters, which is a big deal. For example, when you first name a price, every number that follows in the negotiation compares and relates to yours.

I believe it is best to set the price first. Do not set a price range. If you do, you will start at one end of the range, and your opponent will start at the other end. The person who goes first has a great advantage. Be first. Period.

One other important point: you never know whom you will be negotiating with in the future. Try hard not to burn any bridges. Today's stock worker might be a vice president in ten to twenty years.

During my junior year of high school, my teacher, Mr. Hatcher, gave us a pop quiz. I was a conscientious student and breezed through the questions until I came to the last one. "What is the first name of the woman who cleans the school?" Surely, I thought, this is some kind of joke. I had seen the cleaning woman several times. She was tall, had dark hair, and was in her fifties. Why would I know her name, though? I handed in my paper and left the last question blank.

Just before class ended, one student asked if that question counted toward the quiz grade. "Absolutely," said Mr. Hatcher. "In your careers, you will meet many people. All are significant. They deserve your attention and care, even if all you do is smile and say hello."

I've never forgotten that lesson. I also learned that the cleaning woman's name was Dorothy Watson. It is important that we know the people who are regularly around us. Rank in the business or social pecking order is not important. It will pay off in the long run. It has for me on more than one occasion. Get to know the people you are around.

When you are negotiating, you must know all you can about the people on the other side. At the very least, you need to know their full names. Use their names when you are addressing them. Know the names of everyone—assistants, clerks, everyone on their team. Keep in mind you are negotiating with people who have feelings and personalities. Know your opponent well. That is negotiation's first rule.

What are the different outcomes a negotiation can have for both sides? Here is a chart with the most common outcomes:

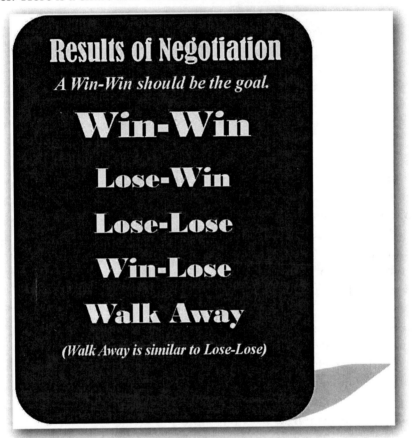

Results of Negotiation

A Win-Win should be the goal.

Win-Win

Lose-Win

Lose-Lose

Win-Lose

Walk Away

(Walk Away is similar to Lose-Lose)

You cannot get along without negotiation—not in the business world or in your personal life. The more you understand this art, the more you will like it—or at least you will tolerate it better. Would most of us be happier without having to negotiate almost daily? Most would say yes. The problem is that negotiation will never go away. It is here to stay. So what is the solution if you want to live happier life? You must learn all you can about negotiation and learn how to enjoy the art of the quest. It sounds easy. As most of us know, it isn't.

Using all my discipline, I have become good at negotiating. Notice that I did not say great. Today, I can go into a negotiation with a smile on my face. I actually get excited when I negotiate. It does get easier. Negotiating is a part of life. You cannot avoid it. Why not enjoy the quest?

A great change agent must have excellent negotiating skills. What other qualities does a great change agent need to have in his or her tool kit?

CHAPTER 15

The Anatomy of a Great Change Agent

The secret of change is to focus all of your energy,
not on fighting the old, but on building the new.
—SOCRATES

A great change agent has many qualities; however, the most important is that he or she is a leader. The true change agent wears many hats and must have many qualities and skills. Here are some of them (in no particular order):

1. An abundance of patience. If it is true that patience is a virtue, then change agents are virtuous.
2. Respect and trust from those he or she is about to lead into change. The change agent should have a solid reputation among all levels of the workforce.
3. Knowledge of change and how to implement it. Being able to handle the pressure of change and change management is a necessity.
4. The ability to accept responsibility for his or her actions. Leaders do not blame others or even imply that others might be the reason for failure. It is not the way change agents do business.
5. Good listening skills. A change agent must learn the art of listening, which requires a degree of patience that not everyone has in abundance.

6. The ability to think outside the box. Being creative is important. Change agents listen to any idea that someone they respect presents to them.
7. Belief in the process. The change agent believes that the pending change is a good thing for the company and its employees.
8. Willingness to stick to the goal and see it accomplished. He or she is not one to lay down the reins when the going gets rough or complicated.
9. Good sales skills. We are all in sales. There is no job that does not require some form of selling. The change agent must be a better-than-average salesperson.
10. Good negotiating skills. During the change-management process, the change agent negotiates several times a day. Negotiating should come as second nature to this person.
11. The ability to make changes to an already-established change plan. Revising a change-management plan is a tricky thing to do well. The change agent knows there should be a written change plan for a revision to an original change plan. These changes can happen several times during the change process.
12. Willingness to take all the time necessary to reach the vision of the change plan. If it becomes necessary to extend deadlines or redo a section of the change plan, the change agent takes the time necessary to get it done correctly.
13. Persistence. The change agent does not stop until the job is done. The word "dogged" comes to mind. In these times and others, the change agent's leadership skills are paramount. The words "persistence" and "stubbornness" are not the same.
14. Leadership by example. He or she does not just dictate orders and commands but gets in the trenches and works with the team until the project is finished. A good change agent is not afraid to get dirty.
15. Knowledge of how to form relationships. The change agent genuinely likes people and enjoys being around them. Getting to know people is a pleasure for him or her.
16. Energy from being with others. You will not find a good change agent sitting in a corner alone on a twenty-minute break. More

likely, the change agent will be talking to large and small groups and having a good time.

17. High integrity. This quality must be there. The change agent has no trouble telling the truth, and everyone takes the agent at his or her word. Integrity brings trust, and every leader must have integrity to succeed.

18. The ability to work well with all levels—from the hourly worker to top management. He or she is at ease with the CEO or the janitor and knows how to communicate properly with each.

19. Self-motivation. The change agent is a self-starter and a self-motivator. He or she does not need to be told when to do something and is often seen motivating others. Change agents have the ability to empower others to do all they can for the team and the process. Giving up power by delegating to others is second nature, as long as the change agent believes those chosen are qualified to do the jobs.

20. The ability to inspire others. An effective change agent considers inspiration a form of leadership. Many times, he or she inspires by being a good example.

21. Leadership experience. This is not the change agent's first rodeo. He or she is savvy when it comes to dealing with resisters and naysayers. Not many things shock the change agent.

22. The understanding that all change causes an emotional response of some kind. A change agent understands the importance of the emotional challenge and is aware that the feelings and emotions associated with change are where success often lies.

23. A positive attitude. The change agent has a positive attitude but can deal with those who do not. He or she never lets someone's negative demeanor affect him or her. He or she might call the employee's attitude into question but is willing to work with all employees who sincerely want to be helped. A good change agent is a positive thinker and is known for treating all more than fairly.

24. Knowledge that change plans do not end when the change is in place. The change agent continues to work until everyone is generally happy with the change. This can take from six months to a year or more.

25. Acknowledgment that change management is a people business. Great change agents know they have opportunities to win or lose with their teams. They do not try to make their jobs anything but what they are—working with all levels of the team to make the change process work as smoothly as possible. They do not try to substitute process for people. The change agent knows it is all about the people.

26. Good preparation. A change agent worth his or her salt is always fully prepared to teach and answer all questions. Being fully prepared earns you respect, and your team will appreciate your efforts.

27. A great sense of timing. Good timing can be a great advantage to the person who understands its importance. When you need to teach something, make sure it is the best time to bring up that particular subject. Know when to praise and when to say nothing. Many times, pausing and saying nothing can deliver a message better than speaking. Silence is a tool everyone needs to use more often in communication. Proper timing will always enhance your ability to keep your audience interested and listening. There is an old story about a middle-aged lady who goes to her family doctor to find out the results of a large series of tests she completed. In the doctor's office, the doctor says to his patient, "I have good news and bad news. Which do you want first?" The lady nervously asks for the good news first. "OK," the doctor tells her, "you unfortunately have only twenty-four hours to live." The shocked patient retorts in a loud voice, "That's the good news! What is the bad news?" The doctor says, "I should have told you yesterday." Timing can make a huge difference.

28. Good delegation skills. The change agent likes to work with teams of people, but he or she knows it is necessary to rely heavily on those teams to get the job done.

29. A team-player mind-set. The change agent understands and promotes the team concept.

30. A strong understanding of human nature and knowledge of what to expect. Change agents are self-taught psychologists, and dealing with emotions does not scare them.

31. The ability to be hard-nosed when the situation calls for it. Change agents are friendly but will not be pushed around.
32. A good sense of humor. An effective change agent knows how to take a joke and tell one.

You know now that a change agent must have in spades what he or she expects the team to possess. A change agent should be a jack-of-all-trades and the master of them all.

However, if the qualities in this list were all job requirements, then no one could qualify as a change agent! No one has all these attributes. The good news is that mastery of a few of the most important qualities is usually sufficient. Good change agents know where they are weak, and they find other team leaders to pick up the slack.

Only a great change agent can make a winning change management team. A great change agent understands the skill of team building.

CHAPTER 16

How to Build a Winning Change Team

Progress is a nice word. But change is its motivator.
And change has its enemies.
—ROBERT KENNEDY

Putting any team together can be a long and difficult task. However, when you get it right, it will put you on a winning track. When you get team building right, winning with positive change will be the norm—not something that just happens once in a while. Winning is almost always a team adventure. More than one leader has said, "A camel is a thoroughbred racehorse put together by a poorly managed team."

The best possible action in team building is to choose your own team members. However, that is not always feasible. For this discussion, let's assume you are not able to pick your team members.

To give you a better feel for the kind of people you want on your team and the type of leaders you are looking for, I offer you some quotes I have put together over the past thirty years or so that I really enjoy reading and thinking about. They are not all about teamwork, however they are positive statements about life and leadership that use the metaphors of the sea and sailing. I hope they also inspire you and bring you wisdom.

Sea Quotes for Land Lovers and Sailors of All Ages

*The pessimist complains about the wind, the optimist
expects it to change, the realist adjusts the sails.*
—WILLIAM A. WARD

If a man knows not to which port he sails, no wind is favorable.
—LUCIUS ANNAEUS SENECA

A boat doesn't go forward if each one is rowing its own way.
—ANONYMOUS

*He that will not sail till all dangers are
over must never put to sea.*
—THOMAS FULLER

Life's roughest storms prove the strength of our anchors.
—ANONYMOUS

The sea finds out everything you did wrong.
—FRANCES STOKES

*He who lets the sea lull him into a sense of
security is in very grave danger.*
—HAMMOND INES

To be successful at sea, we must keep things simple.
—R. D. CULLER

The art of the sailor is to leave nothing to chance.
—ANNIE VAN DE WIELE

*Anchor as though you plan to stay for weeks,
even if you intend to leave in an hour.*
—TOMMY MORAN

Only two sailors, in my experience, never ran aground.
One never left port, and the other was an atrocious liar.
—DON BAMFORD

I find the great thing in this world is not so much where
we stand, as in what direction we are moving—we must
sail sometimes with the wind and sometimes against it—
but we must sail, and not drift, nor lie at anchor.
—OLIVER WENDELL HOLMES JR.

The fisherman knows that the sea is dangerous and
the storm terrible, but they have never found these
dangers sufficient reason for remaining ashore.
—VINCENT VAN GOGH

It is not the ship so much as the skillful sailing
that assures the prosperous voyage.
—GEORGE WILLIAM CURTIS

We must free ourselves of the hope that the sea will
ever rest. We must learn to sail in high winds.
—ARISTOTLE ONASSIS

You cannot sink someone else's end of the
boat and still keep your own afloat.
The water is the same on both sides of the boat.
—FINNISH PROVERB

In calm water, every ship has a good captain.
—ANONYMOUS

An entire sea of water can't sink a ship unless it gets
inside the ship. Similarly, the negativity of the world can't
put you down unless you allow it to get inside you.
—ANONYMOUS

Ships in harbor are safe, but that's not what ships are built for.
—JOHN SHEDD

It is the set of your sails, not the direction of the wind that determines which way you will go.
—JIM ROHM

I suggest you come back to this list from time to time for positive motivation and refueling of your heart, soul, and mind. There is a leadership attitude that these quotes will help you maintain. Enthusiasm is just like the flu; it's catching. Be sure you give it to your team members.

Just as I go into some detail in this book about how to do something, so should you with your team or group. It is better to overeducate a few in the group than not educate the majority of the team members. Here are some good tips that will help you build a winning team every time:

1. Always start on time and end on time. This holds true whether you are conducting your first meeting or any meeting. This is not a small matter. This is important for several reasons:
    a. If the team knows you always start on time, the members are more likely to be there on time. At my office, my team members are usually two or three minutes early. That way, they are prepared from the moment the meeting starts. As team leader, I do the same.
    b. Ending on time allows other team members to plan the rest of their days confidently. You do not hear things like, "Well, you know how these meetings always seem to go on and on." Ideally, team members know that meetings start on time, and they don't stress about meetings running over ending times. Ending on time also forces team members who make reports to stick to their allotted times. All agenda items should have a time limit that the leader establishes. (If possible, the leader and participants should mutually agree to time limits beforehand.) Starting and ending on time will improve meeting attendance, because team members know what to expect. Besides, it is just good manners.

2. Create written vision, mission, and current-reality statements for the group. The group members can contribute their thoughts about all three of these. It is important that team members feel they have ownership of the team's direction.

3. Commit to realistic but challenging goals on the way toward your vision and mission statement for the team.

4. The team leader must be enthusiastic and upbeat. The members of the team will play off the team leader's positive attitude and enthusiasm.

5. Set aside a time for questions and answers at every meeting. This gives members the opportunity to bring up new ideas and talk about the various agenda items that other members have just reported on. This also reduces interruptions to scheduled agenda items. Try not to take any questions except at this scheduled time.

6. Train members in pertinent and needed skills. Decision-making, how to work with a team, and how to handle change are some examples.

7. Lead by example.

8. Send an agenda to each member before the meeting, and note each item's time limit.

9. Appropriate humor is a positive thing at any good meeting. It gets the adrenaline flowing and puts people in a good mood. Keep it clean and lively. The humor should not embarrass any member or be at anyone's expense. Too much humor can disrupt a meeting. Use humor as you would use salt and pepper.

10. As the leader, always stay in charge of your meeting. Overzealous members can attempt to take the meeting over for various reasons. Stay in control.

11. Have only as many meetings as you need. People—including me—generally do not like to go to meetings. Have a full and important agenda, or do not have the meeting. Even if you end it early, it takes effort to attend, and meetings take time away from staff members and the company. The bottom line is to make sure your meeting is necessary.

12. Choose the right location for your team meeting. The room should be well ventilated and noise free. Make sure no traffic will

disturb the meeting. I have seen more than one good meeting with a good agenda ruined by a bad location. Fight for or wait for the right venue.

13. Keep your team members well-informed. When something happens outside of a meeting setting, inform the rest of the team about it as soon as possible.

14. Send out the minutes of the last meeting as soon as they are prepared. If you wait too long, it will be old news. An informed team member is happier and more willing to participate as an active team player. Being well-informed helps with a sense of belonging.

Getting to choose your team members is obviously the best way to build the team you want. However, most of the time, you will not choose the members. Either way, the tips we just discussed should be of help in leading and encouraging a team.

A quality team is the key to making a great change-management plan. Without a quality team the change-management plan is doomed. What is the correct way to build the very best change-management plan?

CHAPTER 17

Creating the Best Change-Management Plan Possible

> *Change means movement. Movement means friction.*
> *Only in the frictionless vacuum of a nonexistent*
> *world can movement or change*
> *occur without that abrasive friction of conflict.*
> —SAUL ALINSKY

have been often surprised that management generally does not know how delicately communication must be treated when informing employees (and keeping them informed) about coming change or ongoing change. A company that puts significant change in place and has a take-it-or-leave-it attitude about that change soon has a staff that vigorously resists—sometimes to the point of rebellion. This is fertile ground for unions. When staff members resist change, it indicates that there is a lack of knowledge and professionalism on the part of senior management. It reveals management's arrogance or even contempt for the employees. Implement change the correct way, and the change can end up being a great success. What is the best way?

You can find sample change plans easily on the Internet. Some will work pretty well, but some are a waste of time. I will give you the change plan that has gone through a thirty-year-long trial-and-error process. After extensive research on the subject, I find that this plan makes the most sense to me and has never failed at any of the companies I own or represent.

Let's us start with the very basics. What is a change-management plan? Here, I'll paraphrase a dictionary definition: a change-management plan is a set of techniques that aid in the evolution and policies to be established for the planned change. It is a detailed map for correctly implementing change personally or in a business setting.

Creating a solid change-management plan is not always hard; however, it does take time and a lot of effort to do it correctly. A change-management plan is the keystone of any organized change. If you get it right, you might still need to adjust your plan—probably more than once. This is a normal part of managing any change. However, it is important to get the original plan as correct as possible. You want to keep changes to it few and far between.

Remember that change involves people, and people come first. If the people involved in the planned change do not feel as if they own the plan for the change, then its chance of success is not good.

The main job of any good change-management-plan leader is to convince people to go along with it. Change agents should openly involve staff members who will be affected by the change in every aspect of the plan and its implementation at every point. The staff must own the plan. If this does not happen, there will be long-term problems with the desired change. You will have trouble with the implementation, and you will have problems with the change after it has been put in place. On the other hand, when you involve the people at the very beginning, throughout designing the plan itself, and in the implementation of the plan, you will reap the benefits of the desired change much sooner.

The church I belong to is presently doing that correctly. The church has held and will hold additional meetings with congregation members about the way we seek new members. That was not the original plan. This was added later, and thanks to these meetings, the members are feeling better about a plan they have not seen yet. In these meetings, those attending were asked for their thoughts and suggestions.

Up to this point, over one hundred suggestions have been made and recorded, and they all will be considered in the final formation of the marketing plan.

Here is a step-by-step process for developing a change-management plan:

1. The leader of the plan must have the trust and confidence of the team or group. That is assured when you choose a person of high integrity and character. It has been said, "Character is a lot like salt; you may not feel it is there, but its absence makes things tasteless, and that thing is discarded." Choose a man of salt. The person chosen must have a high likability factor. This is a major necessary qualification.

2. Explain why your company has to go through this change. Be sure you use language that your group or team will understand. Jack, a shoe salesman, was stunned when the shapely lady he was waiting on stood up, slapped his face, and ran out of the store mad and crying. "What in blazes happened?" roared his manager. "I do not know," replied the very puzzled Jack. "All I said to her was, 'These shoes will make street walking a pleasure.'" Clarity is the key. Think before you speak. Do not sugarcoat the reason.

   Someone a long time ago said, "The truth will set you free." I believe that, and so do all the other experts I know. Showing integrity in the process, whatever the reason for the change, will build trust and acceptance among your people.

3. Write down every part of the plan in detail. The loose rule is this: if you are not sure something should go into the change plan, put it in the plan. Do not cut corners with your change plan. The flowchart below outlines an example of the process for distributing Christmas gifts for one of my businesses. It is not specifically about planning for change, but it does show the detail I suggest you consider in creating a change-management plan. The chart is two pages. I am only presenting the first page as the example:

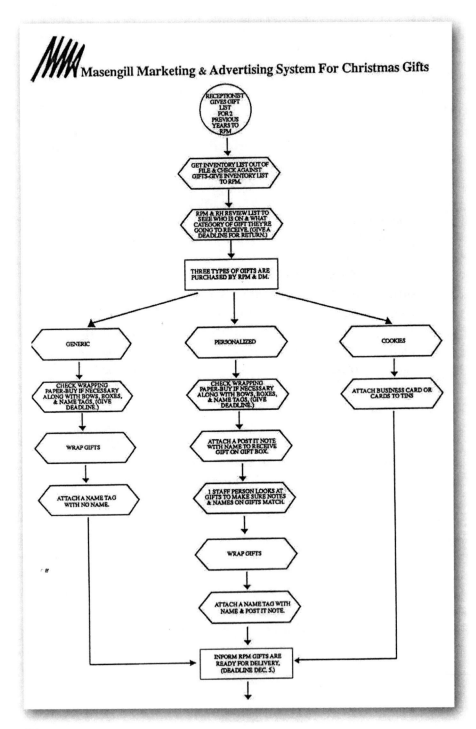

Masengill Marketing & Advertising System For Christmas Gifts

RECEPTIONIST GIVES GIFT LIST FOR 2 PREVIOUS YEARS TO RPM

GET INVENTORY LIST OUT OF FILE & CHECK AGAINST GIFTS-GIVE INVENTORY LIST TO RPM.

RPM & RH REVIEW LIST TO SEEE WHO IS ON & WHAT CATEGORY OF GIFT THEY'RE GOING TO RECEIVE. (GIVE A DEADLINE FOR RETURN.)

THREE TYPES OF GIFTS ARE PURCHASED BY RPM & DM.

GENERIC

PERSONALIZED

COOKIES

CHECK WRAPPING PAPER-BUY IF NECESSARY ALONG WITH BOWS, BOXES, & NAME TAGS. (GIVE DEADLINE.)

CHECK WRAPPING PAPER-BUY IF NECESSARY ALONG WITH BOWS, BOXES, & NAME TAGS. (GIVE DEADLINE.)

ATTACH BUSINESS CARD OR CARDS TO TINS

WRAP GIFTS

ATTACH A POST IT NOTE WITH NAME TO RECEIVE GIFT ON GIFT BOX.

ATTACH A NAME TAG WITH NO NAME.

1 STAFF PERSON LOOKS AT GIFTS TO MAKE SURE NOTES & NAMES ON GIFTS MATCH.

WRAP GIFTS

ATTACH A NAME TAG WITH NAME & POST IT NOTE.

INFORM RPM GIFTS ARE READY FOR DELIVERY. (DEADLINE DEC. 5.)

4. Tell the people involved what is going to be accomplished and when. You must explain each of your goals in the plan until you are confident your people understand and accept the change in a big way. Do not move on until they own the plan.

5. Make sure the team or group knows why you are doing this. It is also important that the team know who you are (your qualifications). Often, this is best told by someone else in your introduction to the group. Make sure you do not let anyone wrongly define you intentionally or by accident, as happened to this unfortunate mother. A mother was struggling to get the ketchup out of the bottle when the phone rang. She asked her four-year-old daughter to answer it. She heard her daughter say, "Mommy can't come to the phone. She is hitting the bottle." Mom heard a click on the other end of the phone. Crazy things like that do happen. Make sure your team or group has the correct information about you.

6. Set clear event deadlines (time and date).

7. Avoid confusion. When people are confused, they become upset and cause unnecessary problems. Do everything in your power to make sure there is little or no confusion. The detail in your plan is designed to minimize confusion and chaos.

8. Do not rush the learning stage of the plan for the team. Give your people more than ample time to understand. Patience is a key. Not everyone will understand and accept your plan at the same time. You should move at the rate of the slowest learners in the group for a while.

9. Be inclusive. Target everyone who will be a part of your planned change in any way. Do not forget even the smallest group or single individual. When done correctly, this will limit the number of resisters you have to deal with throughout the process. Remember the 20-50-30 Rule. Focus on the 70 percent, and ignore the resisters.

10. There's one more bit of wisdom I have learned the hard way. Mark Twain said, "If the desire to kill and the opportunity to kill came always together, who would escape hanging?" Don't argue with someone who likes to argue. You'll only make his or her day and make yourself mad for doing it. Arguing with people hurts

your position. The difference between arguing and discussing is huge. Most of the time, a discussion turns into an argument because of the leader's attitude. Do not argue.

11. Listen. A great attribute of a good leader is the ability to listen. If you do not listen attentively, people will see you as uncaring. Listening also gives you the chance to find out good information. Listening well will enhance your esteem among the group or team, and you can learn a lot.

12. Form a relationship with the group or team as a whole. Also form relationships with individuals in that team. As a change agent, it is your first duty to sell yourself to the stakeholders. (A stakeholder is someone who will be either directly or indirectly affected by the planned change.) It is your job to make sure the majority of the stakeholders are on the change-management team.

13. Monitor every aspect of the change-management plan. If you see anything that is not going as planned, take immediate action. Do not let the situation simmer. Address the area of concern with a written plan, and then follow the plan. Remember that you are dealing with men and women who are all different. They should not be treated the same. Give individual attention when necessary. A cookie-cutter approach will not work for everyone.

14. Negotiate when you need to. A little give-and-take can be very helpful when planning for change. However, do not let negotiating turn into arguing. The change agent must make sure the negotiating team understands at least the basics of negotiation. If the team does not, the change agent must take the time to teach the team members before continuing.

15. Know where you are at all times. Keep an up-to-date record of what is going on while the plan is being put together. Keep detailed records of what has been planned and the attitudes of those on the team or group. This official diary should tell the facts as they actually happen. You cannot continue to plan for change if you do not know exactly where you are in the process. A map is of no value if you do not know where you are on that map.

16. Be a cheerleader. Consistently repeat the good news about the group's planning. If one person or a small team within the

total group does something well, acknowledge that good work. Share the glory. Management of the organization should all be cheerleaders.

17. Have an attitude of gratitude. Thank your people for the work they are doing to put together the change-management plan. Never underestimate the importance of gratitude. It will make both you and those receiving the thanks feel better. Do it often, and do it in public.

18. Move as quickly as possible, but do not rush the process. These two recommendations are compatible; they do not contradict each other. Leaders know the difference between rushing and moving quickly. Most people view change negatively and want to get it over with as soon as possible. When it is finished, begin the implementation stage as soon as it is feasible. There is a tendency to celebrate the finishing of the plan and forget the other actions needed for the finished plan to be successful. Managing change in an incremental way no longer works in today's world—if it ever did.

19. As the change agent, you must be willing to make decisions about what comes first and last and all the details that go in the middle. Having the various parts of the proposed plan in the right places in the timeline is a huge job, and you must give it a lot of thought. The importance of when to do a particular part of the plan is often overlooked or not taken seriously. Getting the parts in the correct order is important.

Here's a story that illustrates the importance of taking steps in the right order:

The Pickle Jar

A teacher stood before her class with several items in front of her. She picked up a huge pickle jar and filled it to the very top with golf balls. She asked the class if the pickle jar was full. The students said that it was. The teacher then picked up a bucket of small, round beads and poured them into the jar until it would hold no more. She shook the jar and then asked again if it was full. The students said yes. The teacher then picked up a jar of sand and poured it into the pickle jar. When she finished, she asked again if now the pickle jar was full.

The students said it was full. The teacher then poured a bottle of water into the pickle jar and filled it to the very top. Again, she asked if the pickle jar was full. The students thought for a minute and then agreed it was full.

The teacher pointed out that the pickle jar represented each student's life. She said the golf balls represented the important things in their lives—things such as God, family, and health. The beads represented other things people care about, such as jobs, cars, and houses. The sand, she said, represented everything else in life. These things are often called the "small stuff." She told her students, "If you put the sand or the water into the jar first and fill it to the top, there is no room for the golf balls or the beads—the things that really matter."

This demonstration shows that if you spend all your time on the small stuff, you will never have room for the things that are important to you. The moral of the story is this: for a happy life, get your priorities in the correct order.

We can apply the same principle to implementing a change-management plan. The order of tasks can be just as critical. Notice that the teacher had one definition of full, and the class had a different one. The students assumed at each stage that the teacher was talking about the jar being full of a specific material or object. We have already discussed how dangerous making assumptions can be—in life and in creating a change-management plan. So how do you make sure your team fully understands that the order of doing things makes a big difference? You ask them questions until you are sure they all get it. Asking questions is a good way to teach as well as know where the team is on the learning curve.

Order counts. Often, one step in the process must be completed before the next step can be started. One step out of order can cause confusion and delay the overall process.

Positive change can be a huge step forward for everyone, so why do most people, at one time or another, see most change as negative? There is such a thing as negative change, but too often, people assume that any change will be a net negative. One reason is that all change, both positive and negative, always causes a feeling of loss. Once you understand how change, whether positive or negative, makes people feel, you can get a better handle on how to avoid being impacted so dramatically by those emotions you and your team will have about change. This might be a good time to go back to chapter 1 and review the definition of change.

When change exceeds what we feel is normal, we react to change more emotionally. Many times, that means we react negatively. If you ask a large group of employees if change is hard for them, most will tell you the truth. About 35 to 45 percent will tell you they do not have problems with most change. They might add that it depends on the kind of change, who must change, and so on. Ralph Waldo Emerson said, "Your actions speak so loudly that I cannot hear a word you are saying." Assess your people based on their actions—not solely on their words.

When you know the facts about change and change management, you know that incorrectly handled change brings serious problems. It is important to properly address the resistance to change you should expect from your group or team. You know the 20-50-30 Rule, and you know resistance comes in many forms. You must address resistance quickly and continuously throughout the plan for change. Ignore the 30 percent of hardcore resisters. The 50 percent, the undecideds, and the 20 percent who are on board are the folks on whose backs you should place large targets. However, many of them will at one time or another during the process have resistant thoughts, and some for a short period may even overtly resist. Remember that feelings ebb and flow. This is normal and to be expected.

Build your change-management plan around these important markers. Each of them will have several subcategories. This is the skeleton or frame to build on. You put the meat on the bones to make the plan yours.

1. Plan to explain more than once the reason for the change. Repetition here is a good thing, as 70 percent or more of the stakeholders must understand the necessity and importance of the proposed change and believe it is the right thing to do over time.

2. Senior management must accept the proposed change 100 percent and be willing to serve as cheerleaders for it and for the change-management plan.

3. All stakeholders, including the change agents, should feel as if they own the change-management plan. Everyone needs to be needed and involved in the planning process.

4. Communication is a major key to success. Getting the messages and news out in a timely way is essential. The group or team must always be in the know. If communication breaks down, revive it quickly. This must have the highest priority.

5. The stakeholders must know immediately that help is available when needed. Those assigned to help individuals and small groups must be accessible and have well-grounded knowledge of what has already happened with the plan.

6. The plan should address any training or retraining needed to make the change plan a success.

7. The attitude and friendliness factors of the change agent are important. Leaders and management sometimes take these qualities for granted, but they shouldn't.

8. Measure progress often. Defined, accurate methods for measuring success are a necessary part of the change plan. Communicate the results of measurements to the entire group quickly. Comfort and a sense of well-being come from knowing where you are and where the team is in the change process. All the tools for measuring and everyone who uses those tools should be spelled out in the change-management plan.

9. Make sure everyone involved understands all the technical terms in the change-management plan. Those terms must be well defined and explained. Include a glossary in the plan. Define words, phrases, and processes there. Do this even if they are defined elsewhere in the plan, and do all this in plain English. To be sure the team or group understands what you have been discussing, ask leading questions. A schoolteacher asks a history class of ten-year-olds, "Which hand does the Statue of Liberty have over its head?" A student immediately says, "The one with the torch in

it." Sometimes you will have to ask the same question more than once to get the real answer.

10. Track all decisions in a decision log. Do this especially for those changes that cause the change-management plan to be altered. The log should be a history of how decisions were made, who made them, and the reasons offered at the time for making each.

11. Include a section in your plan on how you will handle bad behavior. After all, this happens in every change-management plan and implementation. Plan for it. This does not apply only to the 30 percent, the resisters. Bad behavior can be displayed by anyone on the team. Be ready when it happens, and get it under control as quickly as possible. Never let one or two people poison the well. Stop these people as professionally and lovingly as possible, but stop them quickly. Examples of bad behavior include being obvious about not supporting the plan, making snide comments, interrupting a change agent or core team member with negative statements while he or she addresses the team, using sarcasm, missing meetings and deadlines, and talking loudly during a presentation. You have probably thought of three or four more while reading this short list.

Skimp on the planning or implementing side, and your odds for lasting success are small. Proper planning is the first step. It is just as important as the implementation of the plan. It takes two to tango. Get either one wrong, and you might have to start all over. Do not try to cut corners; it will not save time, effort, or money in the end.

Formulating a successful change plan is time-consuming, and it requires patience. However, you will find that it is worth the blood, sweat, and tears.

All excellent change-management plans must have a current reality, mission, and vision statement. How do you create and develop these essential tools?

CHAPTER 18

Vision, Mission, and Current-Reality Statements of the Change-Management Plan

The only way to make sense out of change is to plunge into it,
move with it, and join the dance.
—ALAN W. WATTS

should point out that the vision, mission, and current-reality statements for the change-management plan should never conflict with the vision, mission, and current-reality statements of the company or your personal values. If the company or organization does not have these tools, creating them for the company should be step one of the change-management process.

Vision and mission statements are well-known in the business world. The current-reality statement is less known but still very important in establishing the vision and mission. It's important to have a good idea of where you are today before you can plan for tomorrow. In each of my companies, we have a current-reality statement to work from when we are bringing the vision and mission statements into existence. A map does not provide much help if you do not know where your current location is on that map. Your current-reality statement gives you that, and once it is in place, you can write the company's vision statement and mission statement.

Current-Reality Statement

A current-reality statement tells you where you are today. Data for this statement come from your financial records and other areas (e.g., profit-and-loss statements, balance sheet, total capacity of current facilities and inventories). This document might not be for general circulation (for competitive and security reasons, among others), but you need to know where you are before you can plan where you want to go. I have found the current-reality statement to be a very valuable and necessary tool. You might be surprised at how many companies have never even thought of making a current-reality statement.

Vision Statement

A vision statement is a short, well-crafted description of where you want your business to be in the future. It should be concise but inspiring and speak positively about the future. This helps paint a clear picture of the direction in which you want the company to head. I have seen statements of vision so broad and noble that what they espouse are not goals but ideals. By definition, an ideal is worth pursuing but is not actually attainable. What you write in your vision statement should be accomplishable over time.

Here are some sample vision statements:

Coca-Cola: To achieve sustainable growth, we have established a vision with clear goals:

- Profit: maximizing return to shareowners while being mindful of our overall responsibilities.
- People: being a great place to work where people are inspired to be the best they can be.
- Portfolio: bringing to the world a portfolio of beverage brands that anticipate and satisfy people's desires and needs.

Microsoft: A computer on every desk and in every home, all running Microsoft software.

Disney: To make people happy.

Nike: To be the number one athletic company in the world.

Heinz: The world's premier food company, offering nutritious, superior tasting foods to people everywhere. Being the premier food company does not mean being the biggest, but it does mean being the best in terms of consumer value and customer service.

Ford: To become the world's leading consumer company for automotive products and services.

Avon: To be the company that best understands and satisfies the product, service, and self-fulfillment needs of women globally.

Sony: To become the company most known for changing the worldwide poor-quality image of Japanese products.

General Electric: To become number one or two in every market we serve and revolutionize this company to have the strengths of a big company combined with the leanness and agility of a small company.

For my personal taste, some of these are too short, and others are too long. However, all are appropriate. A vision statement can be a paragraph or a simple phrase or sentence. Your vision statement should fit your company culture and its unique personality.

A solid vision statement is needed to guide management and staff in planning. All the employees of your company should know what the vision statement says and how to explain its meaning and purpose.

Here are the steps for creating a solid vision statement:

1. Enlist as many people as you can on the quest for your vision statement.

2. Give the group or team money or any other tools needed to help accomplish this important project. This includes permission to do it on company time.

3. Ask the group or team to brainstorm about what the vision statement should say. This brainstorming should be done as a group.

4. List all the attributes, virtues, and codes of conduct the company currently operates under. Talk about the integrity and character

of the business. Ask the group these questions: What are the values the company believes in today? What is the legacy the company wants to leave?

5. The vision is all about what the company should strive for in the present and the future. Take time to dream and explore what you want people (especially your customers) to say about the company in the future.

6. You are planning the future direction of the company. Write the vision statement in the present tense, as if you have already achieved the vision. This is important.

7. Do not talk about how you will get to that vision. That is what the mission statement will do.

8. It is important to honor the emotions and feelings you and the group have about the company. In the process of formulating a vision, let the group members express their emotions openly and without recourse of any kind.

9. Your company's vision statement should be somewhat inspirational, describing the best possible outcome in language that employees and customers can understand. Formality is not needed or desired. Paint a pleasant image with a colorful brush, and choose your words carefully.

10. Review your vision statement at least quarterly. In today's world, it can quickly go out of date and be out of sync with what needs to happen. Do not be afraid to adjust your vision statement. This is normal, and it will let your customers and employees know you value this document highly.

11. Once the vision statement is in place, it should be referred to in all business planning from then on.

A well-designed and well-implemented vision statement is an excellent management tool. It helps establish the direction the company should pursue. I have also seen the vision statement used in marketing and advertising campaigns with great results. When fellow workers want to know where a company is going in the future, I tell them to go over the vision statement and give it some real thought. Then we talk about it together. This has worked well for me.

A vision statement can help those involved in strategic planning stay on track. In today's world, a vision statement is a necessity—not just something that sounds good and then goes into a drawer somewhere to be read at the annual meeting of the stockholders. It is a management tool that competent management insists on having and uses often. Everyone in your company should be able to explain the vision statement without having to read it. A vision statement is a great tool for change-management.

Mission Statement

The vision statement and the mission statement are not the same; they have different purposes, but they might sound similar. In the simplest of terms, a vision statement tells you where you are going, and the mission statement tells you how you will get there. There are other differences as well. The mission statement should be about what you do. It should directly or indirectly talk about how to accomplish the company's vision.

Here are some examples of mission statements:

Disney: We create happiness by providing the finest in entertainment for people of all ages, everywhere.

eBay: eBay's mission is to provide a global trading platform where practically anyone can trade practically anything.

Amazon: To build a place where people can come to find and discover anything they might want to buy online.

Google: To make the world's information universally accessible and useful.

Sony: To experience the joy of advancing and applying technology for the benefit of the public.

Ford: We are a global family with a proud heritage passionately committed to providing personal mobility for people around the world.

Toys "R" Us: Our goal is to be the worldwide authority on kids, families, and fun.

Virgin Atlantic: Safety, security, and consistent delivery of the basics are the foundation of everything we do.

The best way to get started on creating your mission statement is to ask yourself and your team questions about the business. Here are some examples:

1. What do we want our image to be?
2. What do we do to earn a living?
3. Why are we in business?
4. What makes us different from our competitors?
5. What are our core values?
6. How do we make a profit?
7. Based on surveys and feedback, what are our customers saying about the company?
8. How can we best accomplish the vision statement?

Getting the mission statement right takes some time; do not rush through just to get something on paper. Involve as many people as possible, and listen to their suggestions. This will allow your staff to feel part of the mission statement's birthing process. It will also give them feelings of ownership. In my experience over the years, the suggestions offered by the staff and team members have generally been excellent.

The mission statement is a very important document and should be used in all business planning. It is usually no longer than a paragraph. A couple of sentences is preferred. There is no one-size-fits-all approach for a solid mission statement that can make a difference.

Here are the steps to forming a mission statement. Ask the staff for suggestions. You will get some good ones. Choose as diverse a team as possible to write it. Explain in detail the purpose of a good mission statement and the process you are using to generate it. Take questions, and make sure the team understands what they have been asked to do. Explain what you want, and ask questions.

1. Ask the team to brainstorm ideas about what needs to go into the mission statement. Write all good ideas on a whiteboard, and leave those ideas up for a while. That way, group members can

review them. (You could also print a handout of them or send an e-mail with the data.)

2. Include the day-to-day things your business will need to do to succeed, be number one in its market, and accomplish the vision statement.

3. Create the vision statement first. You will use the vision statement as a tool in constructing the mission statement. The vision is where you want to be in the future. The mission statement is what makes that happen.

4. Remember that the good ideas you want to express do not all need to be mentioned specifically but can be implied with a sentence or phrase. However, the overall message should be crystal clear. You should not have to think about the statement to get its message.

5. Make the statement pithy. It needs to be catchy, short, and understandable. It is a tool that is sometimes used to persuade customers to do business with you. You are not composing a sonnet.

6. Make sure the statement is uniquely yours. The mission statement needs to belong to your company alone. Every word in it should mean something or say something about your company. Do not use hackneyed or generic phrases or sentences.

The process of creating a current-reality statement, vision statement, or mission statement and the process for creating a change-management plan are very similar. Your company should have these three tools in the company toolbox to use for any change-management plan.

How many in your company can tell you what the vision for the company is without reading it? How many of your employees have actually been given copies of the vision and mission statements? If your team does not know where it is going, it is lost. In *Alice's Adventures in Wonderland*, Alice comes to a fork in the road and asks the Cheshire Cat what she should do. The cat replies, "Where do you want to go?"

Alice answers, "I don't know."

The cat says, "Then either road will do."

The staff of any company feels more confident and content if they know where the work they are doing for the company is going to take the company.

In a personal situation, your family, for example, should know the core values they are being asked to live and operate under. I know families that have a vision and mission statement posted on the family bulletin board or on the refrigerator.

Along with the vision and mission statements, every company should have a current-reality statement. This tells you where you are right now, and it tells you in real time. It is the same in a business or in your personal life. Until you know where you are today, you cannot properly make plans for the future.

The charts below show how you should look at these three important tools for running your business. Study them. First, create the current-reality statement that shows where you are today. Where you want to go is the next step. That's the vision statement. It is important to get these two finished before you go on to the mission statement, or how you are going to get to your destination. Create these one at a time. Often, managers—notice I did not say "leaders"—attempt to do two or even three of them at once. This does not save time. In fact, it could create a near disaster. It does not work. One statement feeds into the other. How can you create a mission statement if you do not know the vision for the company?

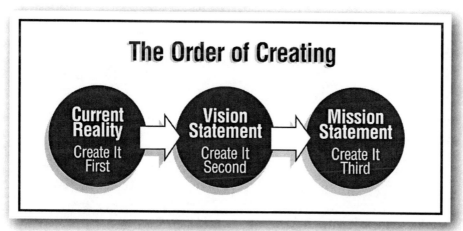

The Order of Creating

Current Reality — Create It First → Vision Statement — Create It Second → Mission Statement — Create It Third

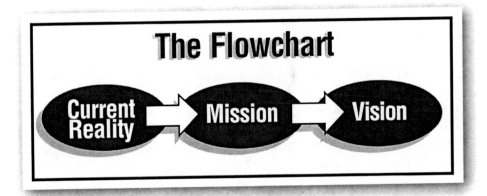

The Flowchart

Current Reality → Mission → Vision

Once you have established where you are, how you are going to get there and where you want to go, keep in mind that you should always expect to make adjustments. What is the best way to do that?

CHAPTER 19

Changing the Original Change-Management Plan

He who is not every day conquering some fear
has not learned the secret of life.
—Shannon L. Alder

New issues and problems can arise as you implement your change-management plan. You might also find that you need to add something new or change something in the original plan. You do both actions the same way.

When you make a change in your plan, you need a separate change plan for that operation. This might sound like overkill. It is not. You must have the discipline to plan in detail the change to the original plan or the original implementation plan. This is important and often overlooked. Get this right, and keep both on track (but perhaps with a revised deadline). If you get it wrong, either one or both could fail.

Research and study the facts. Take changes to either plan seriously. It is not a small thing to adjust a change-management plan or an implementation plan. Here is what you need to do:

1. A well-considered change to either plan should be your first priority. Nothing else should happen until the change is finished.
2. Research whether the change is necessary for the success of either original plan.

3. Make sure the team and everyone affected is involved at every step of your efforts to change either plan. People involvement is a key to success.
4. Use the same processes as when you established the original plan. Do not cut corners. Take the time to do it right.
5. Make the change as quickly as possible.

Changes to a change-management plan or an implementation plan are not unusual. The market might change, or your competitor might roll out a new tactic. There might be some other good reasons to change course. Remain aware of this possibility from the very beginning of your change process, and let the team members know about it. As long as you give the proposed change the time, money, and effort it needs, it should run smoothly. You are changing a process that affects the entire team and the outcome of the original change plan or its implementation plan. This means that the company will be directly affected by what you do.

These kinds of changes can cause some to lose enthusiasm. Keep an eye on the spirit of the group or team. You might be changing a part of the plan that several team members spent a lot of time on. It might be necessary for the change agent, some team members, and management to become cheerleaders for a time. Be sensitive to the overall morale of the team, and adjust. Perhaps something as simple as presenting a couple of funny one-liners could be a good place to start. Here are a few I have used over the years:

- If I've told you once, I've told you a million times: don't exaggerate!
- A retired husband is often a wife's full-time job.
- He who laughs last thinks slowest.
- I went to a bookstore and asked the saleswoman, "Where's the self-help section?" She said that if she told me, it would defeat the purpose.
- Is there another word for synonym?
- What was the best thing before sliced bread?

- Campers: nature's way of feeding mosquitoes.
- The sole purpose of a child's middle name is so they will know when they are in real trouble.

Clean smile humor is always a good tool to use to help keep the group or team listening, and it helps promote a good attitude among the team or group. But do not overdo humor.

Any direct change to the change-management plan should be seen as important as the change to be accomplished by the agreed-to change-management plan. The same is true for an implementation plan. This is not a small thing. This all requires the team or group to go through even more direct change, and we know that change always creates a feeling of loss. The group or team members will have the same emotions as anyone else.

Once you have made all adjustments and changes, it is time to implement the plan. Here is how to do that.

CHAPTER 20

Implementing the Change-Management Plan

Change almost never fails because it's too early.
It almost always fails because it's too late.
—SETH GODIN

Now that you know the ins and outs of making a written change-management plan, how do you implement it? I have found that there are three pillars of change success. One is a correctly written change-management plan. The second is the proper implementation of the written plan based on a solid written implementation plan. This is always difficult. It requires patience, knowledge, good communication skills, an understanding of how to form relationships, and the wisdom and courage to lead from the front.

The change agent who implements the written implementation plan will usually not be the same change agent who is in charge of writing the change-management plan. Some companies agree to let the workers design a proper change-management plan but insist that management implement the change-management plan. This is a mistake. It is a gigantic mistake. It will not work well and will cause discontent in the ranks. Do not let this happen. Let staff members do the writing and implementing.

The third pillar is the 100 percent support and backing of the company's entire management team. They should be cheerleaders for the project. These cheerleaders are not directly involved in implementing the written plan, but from the sidelines, they encourage the change agents and the entire change team in the formation and implementation of the change-management plan. The people in charge of planning and implementing the change plan will not get the job done unless they believe that management is 100 percent for this project and with them all the way. Here are the pillars in chart form:

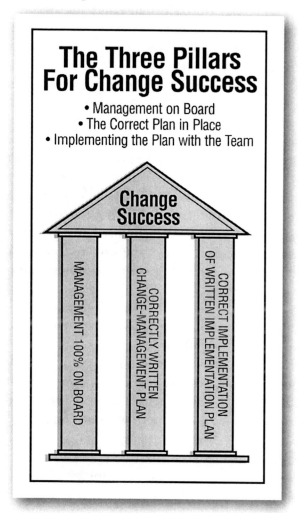

If one of these three pillars is missing or is mishandled for whatever reason, the change process will be flawed and will not be successful. Ensure that these three pillars are rock solid before you start implementation. The chart shows that a weak or missing pillar will cause the roof to fall in on itself.

For change success, a change agent also needs to be flexible. It is important to always be aware of the company's marketplace. The leader and the core team must be flexible and make adjustments based on new market trends and other facts. Flexibility and putting a written, detailed plan into action might not seem to go together, but they do. Flexibility is often one of the keys to final success.

Make sure that stakeholders (those the change will affect directly and indirectly) are part of the team from beginning to end. Here are twenty-eight important tips on how to best implement a change-management plan.

1. Ensure that all of management (that is, 100 percent of management) is on board with the planned change. Management members must openly say so in a language that the stakeholders can appreciate and understand. I have often asked members of the management team to tell the following story about themselves. It helps break the ice between the workers and top management. It will make management seem more human and open to staff:

   > A crow was sitting on a tree, doing nothing all day. A small rabbit saw the crow and asked him, "Can I also sit like you and do nothing all day long?" The crow answered: "Sure, why not." So the rabbit sat on the ground below the crow and rested. All of a sudden, a fox appeared, jumped on the rabbit, and ate it. What can we learn from this story?
   >
   > To sit and do nothing, you must be sitting very, very high up.

2. Constantly keep employees (stakeholders) informed about why the change is necessary.
3. Ensure that the stakeholders believe they own the change-management plan and its implementation.
4. After the implementation is complete and the change is in place, make sure those affected (the stakeholders) still believe they own

the implemented change plan. There should be harmony and a sense of accomplishment for all involved.

5. To quash rumors and trash talk about the impending change, keep the communications consistent and friendly. Communication should be open both ways.

6. Continue to communicate the positive differences that are taking place because of the change. Do this for about six months after the change has been in place.

7. Throughout all these processes, always tell the truth to all the employees—especially the stakeholders. Staff must be able to trust you.

8. Be proactive—not just reactive. When you see a situation developing that can lead to the anticipated change becoming a real issue, you should take action.

9. Identify barriers to the change. Barriers can come from many different sources or departments. They can also come from individuals in the 70 percent group. Resistance might not all come from the 30 percent of resisters. Management might have to deal directly with resisters if they become serious barriers to success. You should ignore the core resisters (the 30 percent). But some resistance is likely to come from within the 70 percent. Usually these folks can be brought back into the fold. However, if they become hardcore, you must act to remove these people from the 70 percent group and place them with the 30 percent of core resisters who are being ignored. Do not delay your action. The moment you have made your decision, you immediately need to take the corrective action.

10. In all these stages, make time your friend. Be willing to overly explain, and do it often. Of course, you do have deadlines. In the case of change, sometimes moving a deadline forward rather than having the team not understand the next process is the best course. You must move at the pace of the team's understanding and level of buy-in. If you insist on meeting the original deadline without waiting for a complete buy-in, you might find you have caused confusion, and that can lead to failure.

11. Party, party, party! Celebrate all successes, small and large. This is a tremendous morale builder. Let the whole team enjoy the successes of others involved in the project. Give out awards (money, time off, gifts, a party in the team's honor, and so on). Awards can be given to individuals, team committees, or the entire team. The important thing is to have fun. Yes, have fun at work on company time. Do this both on and off the company campus. This might not sound like a big thing, but it is. Everyone likes recognition and rewards. Management should also be directly involved in celebrating the team's success. It pays to do this regularly. Again, have fun, and give the glory to the ones who have made it happen. If you do not like parties, then fake it. They are important.

12. Implement the process as quickly as possible. Time is valuable. However, the best way to implement a change movement (in business and in life) and accomplish a goal is sometimes to use your head—not your ego. This means you might have to wait. Waiting can sometimes be the fastest way to real and meaningful success. You need to have a balance between getting the plan implemented quickly and having the patience to make sure the team members understand how to implement the plan correctly.

13. Use the stick approach. In preceding points, we have discussed the carrot approach. Certain team members might require some well-thought-out tough love. We already know that negative motivation is more impactful than positive—if only for a short time. So why do we ever use positive motivators? Because there are far more negatives that go along with the stick approach. Negative motivation is very short-term, while positive motivation can be long-lasting. I suggest you use negative motivation only as a last resort. It can be anything from a soft reprimand to firing someone. Start with the softest stick, and move up the ladder slowly until something works.

14. Provide aftercare for the implemented change. The job of the change agent is not finished once the change is fully implemented. It is still necessary to keep all stakeholders informed about the change. Keep the team up-to-date on how the change has

made and is making a positive difference. If things go well, you'll have a party and celebrate. If the results are not as planned, fully explain why to the group. Tell people you are considering major adjustments in the change-management plan. Let the team know what the company learned from the failure. If you know why the original plan failed, tell them. Be completely accountable for the failure. Do not ever blame the team. It is extremely important to tell the truth about the negatives and the positives. Solid, regular, and consistent communication is important for at least six months after the plan is in place. Many companies continue with positive communication for eighteen months to two years.

15. Why does a change-management plan sometimes fail? We can all learn from our mistakes. However, it is an expensive and painful way to learn. Let's take a look at some of the often-made mistakes.

   a. The sponsors of the change—management—were not enthusiastic. This reason is common. If leaders do not convince the team that they are excited about what the change will mean for them and the company, why should the employees go along with the pain of changing at all?

   b. The team is not given the budget it needs to make the change happen.

   c. The team is given insufficient tools to make the change happen. It is important that the team get the resources it needs.

   d. Communication between the change agents, the team, and team members is not handled in a planned, consistent, and clear manner. Communication is a key to the success of a change-management plan's implementation. Poor communication can bring it all tumbling down.

   e. Management and the change agents have not told the truth.

   f. There is a lack of respect for the management or change agents.

   g. Corrections to the original change-management plan were not handled correctly.

   h. Management fails to celebrate and give the glory to the team.

16. Clearly establish where the overall accountability for the plan and its implementation lies. This is important. Unfortunately, it is not often done correctly.
17. Make accurate assessments, and measure the results for each section of the change plan and the implementation plan. Tell the team what you find.
18. Keep a record of the morale of each team, group, or committee. Also keep a record of the morale of the overall change-management team and the implementation team. If you find that morale is lagging, work immediately to improve it. Go into cheerleader mode. Be sure to insist that management be a part of this action.
19. Look for root causes. If you have trouble completing a section or part of a section of the written change plan, quickly determine why. Take time to find out the real reason for the delay or problem.
20. Keep a positive attitude. I cannot overstate the importance of attitude. The failure to address a less-than-positive attitude is number one on the list of things that can cause a plan to fail. If you have more than one issue, always fix the team attitude first.
21. Be aware that some employees, management included, might attempt to sabotage the plan intentionally. They might delay things just because they are the squeakiest wheels. Whatever the reason, these people must be brought back on board quickly or eliminated.
22. When your change plan is successful, keep all the data and the plan itself in a secure place. That way, you will not have to reinvent the wheel the next time a change is necessary in the company. Change plans are tailored to specific changes, of course, but a previously successful plan provides a general map to work from. That makes the next change process easier and more efficient. Do the same thing for your implementation plan.
23. Choose a meeting place that works. It is best to have your meetings on the company campus (premises), if possible. However, I have found over the years that manufacturing businesses, for example, often have no place to meet with the entire change group or even the subgroups or committees. Meeting off the company

campus can work, but it does take up more staff time. You need a quiet room. (Again, this can be hard to find in manufacturing facilities and some businesses.) You do not want to have to compete with distractions, such as foot traffic or noise. Your job of communicating the change message is tough enough as it is. Give yourself every advantage possible. Make absolutely sure you have a good communication or speaker system. Your great presentation does not matter if the team cannot hear you clearly. Spend the time, effort, and money to make sure the meeting area sends the right message. For instance, don't meet in a dimly lit, stuffy basement.

24. Always speak in the language of the audience. Your team won't understand any message if it's in the newest fad words and phrases. Speak to the average educational level of the group. Use models and examples. At every opportunity, reassure your audience by telling success stories about other companies that have been involved with change. For example, "ABC Company's change was in place within six months. The sales and profits went up, and the company did not have to lay off anyone. That was two years ago, and it's still the case today." Endorsements and testimonials should come from people the change team knows and respects. Testimonials and endorsements are a reassurance of quality, and they encourage listeners to go along with the change plan.

25. Remember that respect is a two-way street. Yes, employees and management should respect and trust the leaders of the change movement in progress, but you must first trust and respect your team members and management. Part of the implementation plan should be to continue to communicate your respect for team members. Be sincere, and do it often.

26. Delegate, delegate, delegate. As a change agent, whether from the management side or the general employee side, your job is never to micromanage. Spread the responsibility. Spread around the decision-making and other aspects of getting the job done. This way, all employees feel they are contributing and have ownership.

27. Focus on the results. Discuss the vision and mission statements of the project and of the company often. I always begin meetings by stating them, and I suggest you do the same. For me, this focuses us in the right direction. The ultimate goal of every activity or action in the company is to accomplish its vision. The mission statement tells people how to get there. Sometimes people get so involved with the details that they fail to focus on the prize, the vision. You must know where you want to go and how you are going to get there.

28. Listen. There is no good communication if there is no listening. Some people see communication as using voice tone, body language, and words to tell an individual or a group something of value. Many take courses on doing that well. I wonder how many have taken good courses in listening. People forget about this learned skill. Many experts say that listening is the greatest communication art, and I agree. Spend more time listening. Some people actually believe they do not have time to listen. Of course they do. Say less. Listen more. Again, the greatest communicators listen 81 percent of the time and speak 19 percent of the time.

One morning, I asked my friend Fred if he would like to get a cup of morning coffee with me. He said no and smiled. He needed to go to the nursing home to eat breakfast with his wife. I inquired about her health, and he told me she had been at the home for a while. She has Alzheimer's disease. I asked if she would be upset if he was a bit late. He replied that she no longer knew who he was. She had not recognized him in five years. I was surprised and asked, "Why do you still go every morning? She doesn't even know who you are." He smiled as he patted my hand. "She doesn't know me, but I still know her."

I've never forgotten this story of love and loyalty. Character counts, and relationships matter in today's world. Some say that people demonstrate less character today than in the past. I do not agree. People want to form relationships with men and women of integrity. If you are a team leader, stay aware of this daily. Tell it like it is. Do not embellish or understate. Tell the truth very well. You will never regret it. Character is one of the pillars of leadership, and it leads to lasting relationships.

Once you have your plan and have implemented it, now we must manage what we have put in place. Some people make the mistake of believing that once the plan is implemented their job is done. That is not the case.

CHAPTER 21

Managing Change Management

The world as we have created it is a process of our thinking.
It cannot be changed without changing our thinking.
The measure of intelligence is the ability to change.
—ALBERT EINSTEIN

et's discuss how to manage change management. If you do not have a written plan to manage change management, failure and out-of-control pain from change are almost certain.

Change management in my opinion is the people process of using specific techniques or tools to effectively institute a shift in the way something is done within an organization and/or change the attitude within an organization. I would like to say again that change management is all about people. The trust you must have needs to be demonstrated on a regular basis by the actions of the change agents and leaders. It is the only way. Here is an example of how a person did in fact tell the truth but was deceptive to the point of pain for the other person. A young man running for political office in a small town is out campaigning in the local neighborhoods. He approaches a home with a strong, white fence around it. Standing in the front yard is a large dog barking. The young politician yells to the man on the front porch, "Does your dog bite?" The man on the porch yells back, "No, my dog will not bite." The young man opens the gate and starts up the sidewalk, and the large dog promptly bites him. He runs out of the yard and slams the fence gate shut. The politician yells, "I thought your dog did not bite!" He hears these words coming from the porch: "He is not my dog." Deception is sometimes worse than an outright falsehood.

Change management is about convincing groups and teams to go through permanent, positive change. This is not easy. You must be seen as a person of character. Implementing change management in your organization takes a lot of listening and a lot of patience. Change often involves giving up things people are accustomed to having in the organization. I have found that the best thing to do in that situation is to look at the big picture. What will the change accomplish for the group and for each individual in time? Even if you are all for the goal of the change plan, you are not immune to the effects that change has on everyone. Keep in mind that even change supporters suffer the pain that change brings.

Be prepared to make mistakes. In the real world of change management, some of what your plan calls for might not be necessary and should be changed or eliminated. This is normal; it is not failure. Promptly admit your mistake, carefully study the situation, and then quickly make your changes to the plan. Logically, it might not seem to make sense to combine well-thought-out preparation and quick action in a change situation. It does, however, when you realize that you must do both to give the new solution every chance of success.

All good leaders make mistakes—yes, every one of them—fairly regularly. The reason they're still considered good change agents and leaders after their mistakes (even major ones) is that they openly admit to them and immediately study how to fix those situations. Then they do it. Sticking your head in the sand or blaming a mistake on something or someone else simply gets you into a bigger mess. Honesty is the best policy. I have seen so-called leaders defend what they knew were real mistakes. You can imagine the chaos this can cause. Here are some red flags to watch for in a change-management plan:

1. Egos have no place here. All good leaders have egos. Some people have very large egos. However, good leaders do not allow those egos to take charge and make decisions.
2. Change is dictated—not managed. Imagine that a company vice president tells staff, "Today, we are making some permanent

changes that go into effect next Monday at eight o'clock." He or she has a handout with details and deadlines and isn't taking any questions. This is leading by intimidation and indifference to the feelings of the employees he or she manages.

3. A change-management plan does not consider the reactions of those who must change or be impacted by the change. This can include anyone from the president to the janitor.

4. The plan for change is not presented in a friendly tone. A smile and a caring demeanor go a long way in smoothing the way to the finish line. The personality of the change agent is very important but often completely overlooked. A person's credentials might look great on paper, but if your agent cannot bond with the audience and communicate well, pick someone else. Likability counts. Attitude counts.

The following story illustrates what could happen if your change-management situation is misunderstood by the change-team leader or leaders:

A ship's captain inspected his sailors. Afterward, he told the first mate that his men smelled bad. The captain suggested that perhaps it would help if the sailors changed their underwear occasionally. The first mate responded, "Aye, aye, sir. I'll see to it immediately!"

The first mate went straight to the crew and announced, "The captain thinks you guys smell bad and wants you to change your underwear." He continued, "Smith, you change with Galbreath; Gregg, you change with Warner; and Brown, you change with Dale."

The first mate, of course, did not accomplish the captain's goal. He tried, but he had misunderstood the order. Who was at fault? The captain assumed the first mate knew what he meant, and that wasted a lot of time and effort. The captain was at fault. The moral of this story is to never make assumptions.

If you find your plan needs to be tweaked, be willing to make several midcourse corrections (changes). Before you make such a correction, though, double-check. Make sure that spending the time, effort, and money required justifies the midcourse adjustment.

Revisions to a change plan can make everyone fearful. People might lose confidence in the rest of the plan if you do not communicate the adjustment well. Encourage your team members to ask questions. Listen to those questions, and answer them completely. In other words, treat a change or correction to a management plan the same way you handle the overall change plan.

Take corrections seriously. You will be glad you did. Most change agents don't give these corrections the attention they deserve. Psychologically, this can have a numbing effect on your entire group, and it can lower morale.

In one case I am familiar with, morale was so low after about six months that the company scrapped the first plan and started over. This time, the first thing the company did was to go over the existing written plan. They found two more necessary corrections. They communicated these well, and the change was finally put into place. I do believe they had to make one more small correction in the second plan after implementation, but they did things right, and the second change-management plan only went past the original deadline by eight months. Again, take corrections to your change plan seriously. When mistakes occur, and they will, promptly admit them and correct them quickly with a written plan.

CHAPTER 22

Conclusion

In ancient times, a wise king had a boulder placed on a major roadway. Then the king hid and watched to see what would happen. Some wealthy people saw the big rock but simply went around it. No one even attempted to move the stone, even though it was not easy to get around. All finally made it around and quickly went on their way. They all left the stone in place for the next traveler.

A kind and hardworking peasant came along. When the peasant saw the huge rock, he first thought he would just go around it. After looking at the massive stone in the road again, though, he decided to move the stone to the side of the road if he could. After much pushing, dragging, and straining, the peasant finally was able to move the stone off the road. As the kind man was getting ready to continue on his journey, he noticed a leather bag lying in the road where the boulder had been. The purse contained many gold and silver coins, and there was a note from the king. The note said the gold and silver coins were for the person who took the time and effort to move the stone to the side of the road. The peasant learned what many of us never understand. Every obstacle presents an opportunity to improve your condition—in more ways than one.

This ancient children's story was a reminder to me that the so-called easy way is not always the correct road for the best return in your personal life or your business in the long run. We need to study our problems more and do more than put Band-Aids on them. The worst problem I have ever endured in my business life ended up being the best thing that ever happened to me. At that time, I thought it was a major disaster. It was, at that time, but it had a silver lining. It led me to a passion I did not know I had. That business passion has been a real source of happiness, peace, and joy on a personal level. It was also the best business decision I have ever made for increasing my income. It was my decision to get into professional marketing and public relations, and that led me to the study of change. My understanding of change has altered my life in a positive way for some forty years. I have been grateful ever since. I can tell you from personal experience that obstacles properly handled can be the best things that ever happen to you. They were for me.

My hope is that the facts and suggestions in this book improve your life in a personal way as well as on a business level. Understanding change and its effects on people will lead you to more success. Understanding change constantly puts you ahead of the curve.

Change is a mystery to most, and it defeats many. You are now the exception to the rule. You have a leg up on more than 90 percent of the population in the United States and the world. You can now make positive change your friend, and use that knowledge to your advantage in many different ways. With the concepts in this book, you can lead yourself and others to more peace, joy, contentment, and overall success.

You now have the opportunity to be all that you want to be in life. Never forget to enjoy the journey. You now have the advantage.

Appendix

More Quality Quotes about Change

In times of change, the learners shall inherit the earth, while the learned find themselves beautifully equipped to deal with a world that no longer exists.
—ERIS HOFFER

All changes, even the most longed for, have their melancholy, for what we leave behind us is a part of ourselves; we must die to one life before we can enter another.
—ANATOLE FRANCE

If you're in a bad situation, don't worry; it'll change. If you're in a good situation, don't worry; it'll change.
—JOHN A. SIMONE SR.

There is a certain relief in change, even though it is from bad to worse! As I have often found in traveling in a stagecoach, it is often a comfort to shift one's position and be bruised in a new place.
—WASHINGTON IRVING

They must often change, who would be constant in happiness or wisdom.
—CONFUCIUS

For either or both ways all minds are always,
Morning and noon and night, sleeping and waking.
Summer and winter, always, always changing.
—JAMES HENRY

Our only security is our ability to change.
—JOHN LILLY

Progress is impossible without change, and those who
cannot change their minds cannot change anything.
—GEORGE BERNARD SHAW

For the past thirty-three years, I have looked in the mirror
every morning and asked myself, "If today were the last
day of my life, would I want to do what I am about to
do today?" And whenever the answer has been no for too
many days in a row, I know I need to change something.
—STEVE JOBS

God, grant me the serenity to accept the things I
cannot change, the courage to change the things I
can, and the wisdom to know the difference.
—REINHOLD NIEBUHR

There is nothing permanent except change.
—HERACLITUS

Some people don't like change, but you need to
embrace change if the alternative is disaster.
—ANONYMOUS

There is nothing so stable as change.
—BOB DYLAN

Change will never happen when people lack the ability
and courage to see themselves for who they are.
—BRYANT H. MCGILL

There are two kinds of fools: those who can't
change their opinions and those who won't.
—JOSH BILLINGS

I cannot say whether things will get better if we change;
what I can say is they must change if they are to get better.
—GEORG C. LICHTENBERG

A fanatic is one who can't change his mind
and won't change the subject.
—WINSTON CHURCHILL

The world is changing very fast. Big will not beat
small anymore. It will be the fast beating the slow.
—RUPERT MURDOCH

For changes to be of any true value, they've
got to be lasting and consistent.
—TONY ROBBINS

When it becomes more difficult to suffer
than to change…you will change.
—ROBERT ANTHONY

Any change, even a change for the better, is always
accompanied by drawbacks and discomforts.
—ARNOLD BENNETT

I can't change the direction of the wind, but I can
adjust my sails to reach my destination.
—JIMMY DEAN

Never doubt that a small group of thoughtful committed citizens
can change the world; indeed, it's the only thing that ever has.
—MARGARET MEAD

The most difficult thing is the decision to act; the rest is merely tenacity. The fears are paper tigers. You can do anything you decide to do. You can act to change and control your life; and the procedure, the process is its own reward.
—AMELIA EARHART

Without change there is no innovation, creativity, or incentive for improvement. Those who initiate change will have a better opportunity to manage the change that is inevitable.
—WILLIAM POLLARD

When you forgive, you in no way change the past—but you sure do change the future.
—BERNARD MELTZER

Life is a series of natural and spontaneous changes. Don't resist them; that only creates sorrow. Let reality be reality. Let things flow naturally forward in whatever way they like.
—LAO TZU

They always say time changes things, but you actually have to change them yourself.
—ANDY WARHOL

The snake which cannot cast its skin has to die. As well the minds which are prevented from changing their opinions; they cease to be mind.
—FRIEDRICH NIETZSCHE

Some changes look negative on the surface, but you will soon realize that space is being created in your life for something new to emerge.
—ECKHART TOLLE

You never change things by fighting the existing reality. To change something, build a new model that makes the existing model obsolete.
—R. BUCKMINSTER FULLER

It's not that some people have willpower and some don't...
It's that some people are ready to change and others are not.
—JAMES GORDON

A bend in the road is not the end of the road...
unless you fail to make the turn.
—HELEN KELLER

Change is the law of life. And those who look only to the past or the present are certain to miss the future.
—JOHN F. KENNEDY

Once your mind-set changes, everything on the outside will change along with it.
—STEVE MARABOLI

When she transformed into a butterfly, the caterpillars spoke not of her beauty, but of her weirdness. They wanted her to change back into what she always had been. But she had wings.
—DEAN JACKSON

You can't just wish change; you have to live the change in order for it to become a reality.
—STEVE MARABOLI

What people have the capacity to choose, they have the ability to change.
—MADELEINE ALBRIGHT

Life is about moving; it's about change. And when things stop doing that, they're dead.
—TWYLA THARP

Where there is no vision, the people perish.
—PROVERBS 29:18

Growth is painful. Change is painful. But nothing is as painful as staying stuck somewhere you don't belong.
—ANONYMOUS

Change can either challenge or threaten you; your beliefs pave your way to success or block you. It's your choice.
—MARSHA SINETAR

All men and women regard all change—both good and bad—with feelings of loss, and those feelings of loss always create some form of anxiety, anger, or fear.
—RALPH MASENGILL

About the Author

Ralph is an adviser, coach, marketing expert, business consultant, and public-relations strategist. Many words could be used to describe Ralph Masengill, but he prefers to be called a friend—a title he fully expects to earn daily.

Ralph Masengill is one of the original change agents in the United States. Before the quality movement came into vogue, he and his associates were presenting seminars and papers to senior management across the nation on quality and change. Quality improvement always requires change.

He and his team were pointing out that until a business, team, or person was willing to understand and submit to positive change, effective quality improvement and substantial profit enhancement were not probable.

He teaches that understanding change is a positive way to enhance your personal joy, peace, and happiness, and the same is true for your business ventures.

Ralph's life story is one of personal challenge, tragedy, and triumph. His professional career continues to be defined by great success in both the private and public sectors. He brings to the table forty years of professional business experience. His company, Masengill Marketing Associates, has won over 850 national and regional advertising and marketing awards for excellence. He is a graduate of the University of Tennessee and the Edwards Deming Post Graduate School of Quality Control.

He and his wife, Dianne, live near the Great Smoky Mountains in East Tennessee. They have four grown children and seven grandchildren, two dogs (Charlie and Beau), and one cat named Bandit. Ralph enjoys woodworking, sailing, oil painting, and working with his favorite charities.

CPSIA information can be obtained
at www.ICGtesting.com
Printed in the USA
FFOW01n0745061116
28940FF